W9-AEK-904

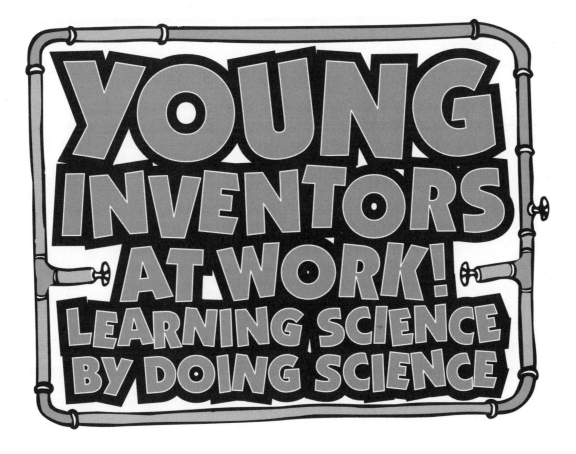

Good Year Books

An Imprint of Addison-Wesley Educational Publishers, Inc.

DEDICATED TO

JERRY VALADEZ AND THE SCIENCE STAFF AT FRESNO UNIFIED SCHOOL DISTRICT AND TO THE TEACHERS AND KIDS AT CARVER ACADEMY AND STONE SOUP

 Good Year Books

are available for most basic curriculum subjects plus many enrichment areas. For more Good Year Books, contact your local bookseller or educational dealer. For a complete catalog with information about other Good Year Books, please write:

Good Year Books
1900 East Lake Avenue
Glenview, IL 60025

Book Design: Meyers Design
Cover and part opener illustrations: Kevin Meyers
All other illustrations: Bill McKinley
Acquisitions Manager: Bobbie Dempsey
Production/Manufacturing Director: Janet Yearian
Production/Manufacturing Coordinator: Roxanne Knoll
Copyright © 1999 Good Year Books, an imprint of
Addison-Wesley Educational Publishers, Inc.
All Rights Reserved.
Printed in the United States of America.

ISBN 0-673-57735-X

1 2 3 4 5 6 7 8 9–ML–05 04 03 02 01 00 99

CONTENTS

CONTENTS

INTRODUCTION

Young Inventors at Work! challenges kids to exercise creative problem solving and critical thinking to design, build, and test model structures, games, and vehicles. Kids work in teams to solve technology-based problems. Their desire to find optimal solutions leads them to discover basic principles of science and engineering. Related science experiments or demonstrations accompany the activities. "Stories for Young Inventors" are intended to be interactive readings to provoke thinking and learning, and to be repeated at home.

These activities were developed for Fresno (California) Unified School District for use as an after-school informal science education program for children in grades 4 through 8. There are twenty-four active activities and twenty-six readings, consisting of original stories about inventors and inventions.

Young Inventors at Work! is suitable as an informal science program for school, youth groups, or home use, and as part of a formal science program at school.

The goals of Young Inventors at Work! are:

1. To fire each participant's enthusiasm for science (physics), engineering, mathematics, and technology
2. To get participants comfortable with technology and the tools of technology
3. To get them thinking, talking, and learning about science and technology
4. To have them learn about and think about role models in science and technology
5. To have them carry home their excitement for learning to share with siblings and other family and friends
6. To spark their creative energies and engage their problem-solving abilities

Young Inventors at Work! is predicated on the following axioms:

- To learn science and technology, kids need to think about science. Scientists and inventors think about their subjects and learn from testing their ideas. For them, learning is an enjoyable experience.
- The way to get kids to think about science is to challenge them to use their creativity and problem-solving abilities to solve realistic problems. Once they have invested their creativity in solving a problem, they will continue to think about and work on the problem, even after the lesson has finished. Once challenged, they become scientists and inventors solving problems and learning.

- Challenges that will engage kids are ones that are intrinsically fun, ones they can complete, ones that require their focused attention, and ones that allow them to apply their knowledge and skills to get something done. Simple challenges and cookbook approaches don't excite a passion to explore.
- The more time a child spends thinking about science and technology, the more he or she will learn, so our challenge is to get kids to continue these experiences at home. If they engage their families in these activities, the learning will infect more people and they may build a family culture of learning.
- To get kids to work on projects at home, the projects must be designed to use tools and materials that are available to most kids. Exotic lab equipment is ruled out.

MANAGEMENT OF THE CREATIVE PROCESSES

Young Inventors at Work! provides a fundamentally different type of experience than the traditional classroom and, to be effective, requires a different style of management. These experiences beg to be led by a facilitator who outlines the challenges and ensures that materials and tools are available, and that safe working conditions exist. Laboratory workers—the participants—seek to solve problems by working in teams with their peers.

These activities encourage teams of kids to find better solutions to fun problems. *Young Inventors at Work!* doesn't offer rewards for meritorious work other than praise for a job well done. Creative failures are as valued as successes, and the facilitator/leader should direct discussions on the design elements that worked or didn't work in each design, as opposed to giving overall evaluations of one group's solution compared to another's. Each team will try to do a better job than the next team, but they should be encouraged to help the next team. Sharing information is an important part of the learning process.

Young Inventors at Work! begs for the services of volunteers to assist the facilitator/leader. There is simply too much to do for one person with 15 to 20 kids. We suggest enlisting older students, high school or college age, or adult volunteers (for example, Telephone Pioneers or other organizations of retired people) to assist as Inventing Guides. Guides can prepare and give demonstrations, read readings, and help teams with their activities. They can also help clean up. You want Guides who will bond well with the teams and help the teams without solving the problems for them. The Guides will become role models, and as such they must exemplify the spirit of *Young Inventors at Work!:* encouraging teams with positive feedback and being helpful, friendly, inquisitive, creative, and industrious. The best training for Guides is to have them perform the activities while you act as their guide, modeling the approach you want them to take.

LESSON MAKEUP

Each lesson description consists of seven components:

1. **OVERVIEW.** This is a short description of the main activity.

2. **OPENING.** Recognizing that not all the kids will arrive at the same time, the Openings provide learning activities for early arrivers. The intention is threefold: one, to get early arrivers engaged in meaningful and fun learning; two, to encourage all the kids to arrive on time since late arrivers will miss the fun of engaging in the opening activity; and three, to introduce the topic for the day.

   The opening of the lesson is also a time to invite anyone who worked on a previous project at home to show what they developed. Please remember to ask if anybody did more work at home. Since *Young Inventors at Work!* is built on the premise that kids will replicate fun activities at home and with their friends, we want to encourage and reward this behavior.

3. **DEMONSTRATION.** Given by a guest, a Guide or the Leader, demonstrations relate to the lesson and often provide concepts helpful for finding a solution. For home or small-group use, demonstrations could be presented as science experiments for the Leader and participants to undertake together.

4. **READING.** The "Stories for Young Inventors" in Section II of this book are intended to be interactive elements of the lesson where questions and statements written in italics are directed to the listeners to engage their responses. The readings emphasize the notion that inventors are people of both genders and all races who overcome adversity to solve problems and that they take advantage of mistakes and opportunities. In most cases, the readings tie in with the activity.

   Copies of the readings can be made available for kids to take home to read to their families. Readings are included in Section II of this book. There are more readings than activities since you may choose to repeat a lesson (for example, you could use Take Apart several times with different materials to take apart, or with different activities built around it). Several of the stories mention specific geographic locations to afford readers the opportunity to use an atlas.

5. **ACTIVITY.** This is the principal component of each part of the lesson. The Leader specifies a problem to be solved and any constraints on the solution. Kids break into teams of two to four, depending on the activity. In most cases, before they are allowed to start constructing a solution, teams must first show a thoughtful design on paper to one of the Guides. The requirement for a design is to force them to think as a team and agree on what they are going to do, rather than having the dominant personality say, "Oh, I know what to do, I'll . . ." to the exclusion of other members of the team. Everyone participates or the team doesn't proceed. It also forces abstract thinking and the comparison of an object with its design on paper.

6. **DEPARTURE.** This is the opportunity for Leaders and Guides to transform home behavior into learning activities. The longer a child works on a problem, the more he or she is likely to learn. By encouraging kids to keep working on the activity at home, Leaders will extend the learning environment and greatly facilitate real learning.

7. **REFERENCES.** Books and articles are listed that may be helpful to you in extending the activities.

OBSERVATIONS

1. Everyone—kids and volunteers—walks into the room and asks, "What are we doing today?" Once people know that fun, creative activities usually transpire, they want to know what's next. We suggest having a "coming events" sign outside the classroom listing today's activity and tomorrow's.

2. We have found that some kids need to see a concrete model of a solution before they can come up with their own solution. When teams are stumped, one of the inventing guides will make a mock-up to show them. Once the participants see it, they can start designing improvements to it.

3. Many of the activities provide wonderful photo opportunities for the media or your own community relations people. Published stories and photos could open up funding opportunities, so you might consider inviting the media.

SECTION 1 ACTIVITIES

TAKE APART

OVERVIEW

Kids love to take things apart, and they can learn a lot in the process. There are at least three types of learning that occur: learning to work with tools, learning to work with each other, and learning about technology. All three types of learning instill confidence and empower kids to ask questions and explore further. A major focus for Inventing Guides is to help kids know where to go to seek answers to their questions and to make sure they know how to do Take Apart safely at home.

A challenge of offering Take Apart is to slow down the process of equipment destruction and get kids to think. Since you might want to offer this activity several times, there are several different activities suggested under the umbrella of Take Apart.

TOOLS AND MATERIALS

Safety goggles (1 pair for each participant), newsprint, pencils. Flat and Phillips' screwdrivers, and pliers for each team. Additional tools to keep in a central location: jeweler's screwdrivers, Allen wrenches, vice grips, needle-nose pliers, and an adjustable wrench. For the Opening: shoe boxes taped shut with common objects (a ball, a large paper clip, a pencil) inside.

OPENING

As kids come in, have several shoe boxes set out on tables. Each one should be sealed to prevent casual opening and each one should have a common object or objects inside.

Challenge the kids to figure out what is inside each box and write down their answers on a piece of paper. They can rattle or shake the boxes, smell them, and feel the weight, but they can't see or come in contact with the contents.

At the appointed start time, ask the kids if they were able to identify what was in each box. Ask them for their ideas before opening each box. Explain that scientists and inventors make educated guesses about things they don't know and then test them (like opening the box) to find out. Many times they are wrong, but that doesn't matter as long as they learn in the process. Science and inventing are processes of finding out.

DEMONSTRATION

Demonstrate the tools for this activity: brainstorming and hand tools. Brainstorming is a technique for individuals or groups to come up with creative solutions to problems. People use brainstorming any time they need to solve a problem. There are only a few rules to follow:

1. Everyone participates. You want different ideas because they can lead to some of the best solutions. Different is good.

2. During the "idea phase," you want to generate as many ideas as possible. They can be silly, bad, or great ideas. Someone writes them all down and no one comments on the ideas (no one says, "That's dumb," or even "That's good").

3. When everyone has run out of ideas, you go to the "deciding phase" in which you look critically at each idea to decide if it will help you solve the problem. You select only a small number to try. You can add to the list if more ideas come along, and you can go back to the list to try more ideas if you want. Coming up with ideas and deciding which are best use different thought processes. To get the best results, the two different activities should be done separately.

Have a Guide show the participants the tools and materials, provide names for the tools, and show the participants how to use the tools and of what they should be careful.

READING

Take-apart King (Charles Kettering), page 110

ACTIVITY

Each time you offer Take Apart, follow this outline:

1. Describe the activity. Identify the pieces of equipment to be taken apart. Stress that nothing else should be taken apart. Describe the specific things you want the participants to be aware of, or to do.
2. Show them the tools they will need. Make sure they know the names of the tools and how they are to use them. You might have one of the Inventing Guides demonstrate the safe use of each tool.
3. Review the rules of Take Apart. Although we encourage kids to break thought-constraining rules (that is, to think outside the box) while they invent, they are not to break Take Apart rules.

Rules for Take Apart:

A. Always cut off the electrical plug on any device you are taking apart. Inventing Guides will help do this. Throw these plugs away where kids can't get to them, or bend the plugs so they can't be inserted into an outlet. Never try to reconnect the devices or fool around with AC electricity.
B. Wear eye protection while taking anything apart.
C. Never point a screwdriver or other sharp tool at yourself or at anyone else. Always point it away from people.
D. You don't need a hammer. The idea is not to destroy the components, but to get them out. Maybe you'll find a part you can use.
E. Never take anything apart unless the owner says it's okay. It's unlikely that you will get it back together again, so if it works, leave it alone. Even if it doesn't work, ask the owner first.

ACTIVITY I

Ask questions about each piece of equipment: What does it do? How does it operate? Where does it get the energy it needs? Where does the energy loss manifest itself? (Does it get hot?) What do you expect to see inside? A motor, a series of electrical components, switches—what else?

Divide kids into teams of two to four, depending on the availability of stuff to take apart. Ask them how their team will function: Will everyone take turns using the tools and asking questions? Will everyone get a chance to help?

Assign teams to particular pieces of equipment and have them send one person to get the tools they need from one of the Inventing Guides.

As each team gets started, have the Inventing Guides wander about to:

1. Make sure the safety rules are being followed.
2. Help, but only where help is absolutely needed. This is not an activity for the Inventing Guides to perform and the kids to watch.
3. Ask questions to get kids thinking. "What is this for?" "Why do you suppose the engineers put this piece in there?" "Isn't this a neat way to do . . . ?" "How could you use this part in your own inventions?"
4. Slow down the urge to hurry. Make sure the activity is Take Apart, not rip apart. The best way to do this is by asking questions. Also, if there is pushing and shoving going on regarding whose turn it is to use a tool, the Inventing Guides should take the tools away until the team can come up with an agreed-upon plan for how to share the workload.

Devote about ten minutes at the end to have a group discussion on how the activity went. You might see whose team learned the most about the machine they were taking apart, and let each team explain what they learned. Encourage participants to take safe components home, but first check for sharp edges, glass that could break, and other dangers. Remind them that although they can do Take Apart at home, they must still follow the rules (review the rules), especially the rule about asking the owner's permission before taking anything apart.

ACTIVITY II

This activity provides a bit more structure to the general Take Apart and is recommended for the second time you offer Take Apart. Ask each team to create a classification system (use brainstorming to come up with the system) for the parts they take out. Their system can have no more than ten classes and no fewer than six. Have them take some newsprint and create large squares for each class. They can pile up the parts in the appropriate squares. They can change their classification system as they proceed. You might suggest that an effective system is one in which there is some equivalency between the numbers of parts in the classes. Teams might classify parts by color, shape, size, material, function (gears, springs, etc.), or perceived cost.

When a team has concluded, ask them to talk about the piece of equipment, how it worked, and the parts they found. They can describe their classification system and show examples of parts in each class.

If there is time, challenge them to come up with an entirely different classification scheme. For example, if they used a functional classification scheme (gears, electronic components, buttons, . . .), they could reclassify parts by size, color, shape, and so on.

ACTIVITY III

The challenge is to make something from the parts they extract. This is a good time to use brainstorming. You could limit them to using only those parts, or allow them to use tape or other materials in addition to the parts they find. They can trade with other teams for parts they want. The results will be fantasy inventions that they can describe to the rest of the group.

DEPARTURE

Challenge them to look at devices (a toaster oven, binoculars, slide projector) and try to figure out what's on the inside. Suggest that they also look for discarded devices for Take Apart, and that they can bring them in for the Inventing Guides to check out before taking apart. Tell them what the activity for the next session will be and ask them to think about it.

REFERENCES

David Macaulay, *The Way Things Work*. Boston: Houghton Mifflin, 1988. This is a wonderful resource.

Robert Gardner, *This Is the Way It Works: A Collection of Machines*. Garden City, NY: Doubleday, 1980.

SPAGHETTI STRUCTURES

OVERVIEW

Kids love to build things, and by using spaghetti they can build and learn with little cost for materials. Building spaghetti structures will challenge their ability to work effectively in teams, to think through problems and apply their knowledge. One of the great features of this activity is that kids can replicate it at home, and you should encourage them to do so with permission from a parent or guardian. (If unable to use spaghetti, substitute drinking straws.)

TOOLS AND MATERIALS

Two large boxes of spaghetti (thick strands) and one roll of 1" masking tape. One tape measure. Newsprint and pencils. Two or three books (for weight). Demonstration: examples of cooked and uncooked food (spaghetti, an egg, rice, cookie dough, etc.).

OPENING

As kids walk in, invite them to design a skyscraper. They can draw their designs on newsprint. Encourage them to draw big by giving them a four-foot-long section of paper. Prompt the Inventing Guides to ask each designer if his or her building will have windows, an outside or inside elevator, or a helicopter pad on the roof, and whether the building will be rectangular in cross section or some other shape. Remind them that really tall buildings have names and they should come up with a creative name for their designs. When you are ready to start the day's activities, ask the Guides to tape each design up on a wall. Review them all, allowing students to comment.

DEMONSTRATION

Explain that today's activity involves building structures out of spaghetti. Then hold up some cooked spaghetti. "What happened to it?" "What happens to food when we cook it?" It changes. Spin a raw egg and a hard-boiled egg. They spin differently. "What happened to the egg when we boiled it?" "What other foods change when we cook them?" Breads and cookies, meat, vegetables, gelatin dessert . . . Cooking changes the chemistry inside the food. "Can you change food back to its precooked state?" No. "Which would be better to use for building: cooked or uncooked spaghetti?" "Today, we'll use uncooked spaghetti instead of cooked spaghetti."

READING

Elevators: How to Get Up in the World (Elisha Otis), page 92

ACTIVITY

This is a team activity (two or three people per team) that will require table space. Make sure that each team has adequate room to build.

One of the pedagogic challenges with Spaghetti Structures is getting kids to think before building, and here are two suggestions. First, have them build a small structure without taking time to discuss it. This will let them "get at it" right away and make some mistakes that they can correct in subsequent activities. Hopefully, they will see good features in the structures other teams are building and will think about how to incorporate them into their design. Second, when they're ready to undertake the main activity, have students sketch their ideas on some newsprint before giving them the materials with which to build.

PRE-ACTIVITY

Pass out seven strands of spaghetti and 1" of masking tape and challenge students to build a structure that won't fall over when one of the Inventing Guides blows on it while another shakes the table. They can't tape any spaghetti to the table, and the structure has to have a vertical component standing above the plane of the table (they can't lay all the strands flat on the table and claim that they're finished). Place a three-minute time limit on this activity.

When the three minutes are up, go to each team's structure and look at it. Ask the other kids what the strengths of the design are and how they think it will hold up. Comment on the use of triangles as a way to distribute force (look for examples in buildings, bridges, and construction toys) and on the precision of the teams' work. Then have the Guides test the structures.

After testing, go over which features were most effective (don't point out whose structure was best; keep the personalities out and focus on the engineering). Point out the use of triangles. If no one used a triangle, make a spaghetti triangle to show how strong it is, and suggest they use triangles to brace their structures.

PRE-ACTIVITY II

Before proceeding, search the room and building for examples of frame construction. Look at how builders strengthen buildings. Suggest that the kids look at houses being constructed to see how the carpenters frame them, looking especially for how they add strength to the building. This would be a good time to show them examples of buildings in books: David Macaulay's *Unbuilding* and Philip Wilkinson's *Amazing Buildings* are two to check on (see the References section of this activity for more information).

ACTIVITY

The challenge is to build as tall a structure as possible out of the spaghetti. Before each team receives the materials (once they have the materials they will start building, so have them think through their design before they start), they must show one of the Inventing Guides how they are planning to build the structure. They need not draw the entire structure, but just show how they are going to connect the spaghetti and brace each level of the structure.

Now give each group 25 strands of spaghetti and 6" of masking tape. They can have as much spaghetti as they need, but no more tape. They cannot tape the structure to the table or use any other materials to support the structure. Give them a time limit, up to 30 minutes.

Provide a five-minute warning that time is running out. At the appointed time ask everyone to stop building. Ask who wants to show off their structure first and explain the design and why they think it is good. After everyone has shown their structure, ask the Guides to measure the structures.

ACTIVITY II

If there is time, give them this second challenge. They are to design a structure that will hold up a book at least 6" off the table. Give them 12 strands of spaghetti and 4" of masking tape. They can't apply tape to the table and they can't use any other materials. If their structure is able to hold a book (you might use David Macaulay's *The Way Things Work*—it is heavy and has a firm cover), it can go into the championship round of testing, in which you add additional books to see which structure holds the most weight.

After all the structures have failed (keep loading them until they do fail), talk about which design features were most effective in holding up the books. Encourage the kids to try this at home with their families.

DEPARTURE

Suggest that they look for triangles in bridges, houses being constructed, and other buildings. Also suggest that they search for materials other than spaghetti to use in building model buildings, and that they should come back next time able to tell everyone what they found that worked. Tell them about the activity for next time and invite them to think about it.

REFERENCES

David Macaulay, *Castle* (1977); *Cathedral: A Story of Its Construction* (1973); *Pyramid* (1975); *Unbuilding* (1980); and *Underground* (1976), all Boston: Houghton Mifflin.

Philip Wilkinson, *Amazing Buildings*. New York: Dorling Kindersley, 1993. Dorling Kindersley publishes several beautiful books showing cross sections of machines and buildings.

Bernie Zubrowski, *Messing Around with Drinking Straw Construction*. Boston: Little, Brown, 1981. This author has published a series of books of activities he developed at the Boston Children's Museum.

MAKING BARGES

OVERVIEW

Messing around in water will delight kids. In this and the following activity, they learn about buoyancy. For the Making Barges activity, each team forms a boat from a piece of aluminum foil, trying to give it the maximum carrying capacity. In the next activity, they will make model boats from half-gallon containers and then add a propulsion system of their own design.

SPECIAL TOOLS AND MATERIALS

A wading pool or other large structure in which to float the boats. A large sink will work. A large measuring cup.

Participants can also design and build a simple trough to test their boats in by making a frame of pine boards and laying a piece of plastic sheeting inside to hold the water. Three pine boards (8' long, 1" x 12") will suffice, with one board cut in half to become the two end pieces. The trough ends up 4' x 8', standing 11" off the ground. Rather than designing and building the trough yourself, have the class do it.

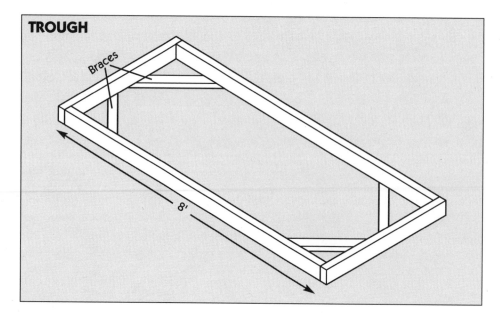

TROUGH

Braces

8'

TOOLS AND MATERIALS

Aluminum foil (1 roll), straws (2 boxes), masking tape (1 roll), scissors (1 pair per team). A two-liter plastic soda bottle with lid. Balloons (1 per team). A pound of nails.

OPENING

As early arrivers come in, give each pair a square piece of aluminum foil (as long as the width of the roll). Challenge them to make a cup from the foil that will allow them to carry the most water. At the appointed start time, have each team take a full scoop of water with their cup, carry it across the room, and dump in into a measuring cup. Have one of the Inventing Guides record the volume of water carried by each team. Examine each of the team-made cups and talk about the strengths and weaknesses.

DEMONSTRATION

If you have a deep sink or tub, you might introduce buoyancy by blowing up two balloons and immersing them in the water. Blow only enough air into one balloon to give it shape and fill up the second one; tie the ends of each. Ask the students which will be more difficult to push to the bottom of the sink. Then have one participant try to push them, one at a time, to the bottom and report to the group which was easier. "Why was it harder to push the larger one down?" The more water an object displaces (pushes out of the way) the more buoyancy it has (the more the surrounding water pushes up on it).

A second buoyancy demonstration is to make a Cartesian diver. In front of the class, take a 2" square of aluminum foil and crumple it up into a cylinder. Drop it into a plastic soda bottle filled with water and screw on the lid. The foil should float, but as you squeeze the bottle, the foil should sink. If not, remove the foil and squeeze it tighter to get rid of some of the air and then retry it. By squeezing on the bottle, you increase the pressure inside, which reduces the volume of air inside the foil. With less air volume, it sinks. (Air is compressible and its volume reduces as pressure increases. Water, however, is nearly incompressible and no matter how hard you squeeze, its volume changes very little.)

READING

Putt-Putt (Ole Evinrude's Outboard), page 106

ACTIVITY

There are two activities that focus on buoyancy. Teams consist of two or three students.

Ask why a boat floats. If someone answers because it is lighter than water, ask them what boats and ships are made of. Some are made of wood, but more are made of steel and a few are made of concrete. Do steel and concrete float? Tell them that a boat is a hole in the ocean that used to be filled with water. The boat is now occupying that hole in place of the water. The boat displaced the water, and the more water it displaces, the more the surrounding water pushes back on the boat. Relate this discussion to the two demonstrations: "Why did the Cartesian diver sink when the air inside was compressed, but float when it wasn't compressed? Why was the larger balloon harder to push to the bottom?"

The challenge is to make a boat or a barge that can carry the maximum load. Ask each team to think about the problem and how to solve it before coming up to get a piece of aluminum foil. Give each a square, equal in size to the width of the foil. They can fold it any way they want to make a boat or barge and can use up to 2" of masking tape. After each team has made their boat, test each in the wading pool by successively adding weight (nails) and keeping count. Examine the boats that held the most nails and discuss the design characteristics.

Buoyancy Extension 1. Let the teams go back and redesign their barges, and give each team five plastic straws to use any way they want. The challenge is to incorporate the straws into a boat to give it greater buoyancy. They can also use 2 more inches of masking tape. Retest the barges. Did the new materials (straws) allow their barges to carry more weight? What other materials could they use to improve their model barges?

Buoyancy Extension 2. Now give each team one balloon and ask them to redesign their barge to hold the maximum number of nails. How can they incorporate the balloon and straws into their barge?

DEPARTURE

Suggest that they could try this at home with aluminum foil and pennies or some other materials. Invite them to bring in their best design to show the class next time. Also ask them to bring half-gallon plastic milk or juice containers (rinsed out) for the next session. Finally, ask them to think about what makes boats go.

REFERENCES

David Macaulay, *The Way Things Work*. Boston: Houghton Mifflin, 1988. Look for an illustrated section on "Floating."

MAKING BOATS GO

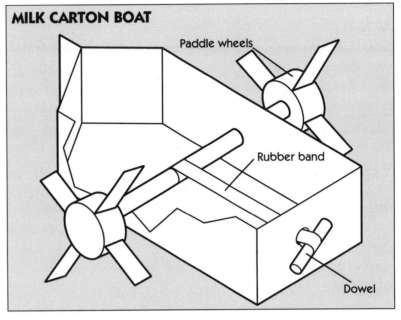

MILK CARTON BOAT

Paddle wheels

Rubber band

Dowel

OVERVIEW

Kids make boats out of half-gallon containers and design and build propulsion systems for them using rubber bands and balloons.

SPECIAL MATERIALS NEEDED

A wading pool or other large structure in which to race the boats. Windup toys. A candle and matches.

TOOLS AND MATERIALS

1/4" dowels (4), half-gallon milk or juice containers (1 for every two teams), duct tape (1 roll), nails (1 lb.), masking tape, rubber bands and balloons (10), straws (1 box), scissors, paper and cereal box cardboard. A saw to cut the dowels.

OPENING

Challenge kids as they come in to make a fan capable of blowing out a candle two feet away. They can use paper or cardboard and not more than 2" of masking tape. The only thing they can use to move their device is one rubber band. In other words, they can't fan their device by hand to blow out the candle. They have to wind up their device and let it go.

When you are ready to start the activity, set up the candle, making sure nothing else flammable is nearby. Invite each team up to demonstrate their device. Talk about what worked and what didn't.

From the last session: Ask if anyone worked on their barges at home and has a new model to show.

DEMONSTRATION

Demonstrate a windup toy. Ask how it moves. It needs energy; where did the energy come from? Where did the energy come from to launch a rubber band across the room? The energy came from you, but it was stored in the rubber band. You got the energy from food, which got its energy from the sun. The farther you stretched the rubber band, the more energy you stored. Now inflate a balloon and let it go. Where did the energy come from? Where was it stored? Propulsion systems need a source of stored energy.

READING
Propel Yourself (John Ericsson), page 104

ACTIVITY
Have the Inventing Guides cut the half-gallon containers in half, lengthwise. Each team of two kids gets one half. If two teams want them to, the Guides can cut the containers on the diagonal to make two V-shaped hulls, instead of two square-shaped hulls.

The challenge is to devise a system to propel the boats. First have participants make a balloon-powered boat. After they try out their first models, ask them if using a straw would help direct the balloon's discharge. Would it be better to vent into the air, or into the water? Would two balloons work better than one? Give them a time limit to complete their boats and to race them across the wading pool. (You might want to use distance traveled instead of speed as the goal since distance will be easier to measure.) After the races, examine each boat and ask the kids to describe which elements of the design worked especially well.

ACTIVITY 2
Ask them to remove the balloons and use a single rubber band to power their boats. How will they use it? They can make side-wheelers, stern wheelers, or a launcher to push their boat from the edge of the pool. They can use a dowel as the axle for their paddle. Have participants sketch their design before starting to build their new propulsion system. Test them at the end of the lesson period. Which design went farthest? What made it successful?

DEPARTURE
Suggest that they could make more models from recycled stuff and try different propulsion systems in their bathtubs at home. Ask them to report on their experiments at the next session.

REFERENCES
Barbara Eichelberger and Connie Larson, *Construction for Children*. Menlo Park, CA: Dale Seymour Publications, 1993. The authors include several fun projects for propulsion toys.

George Pfiffner, *Earth Friendly Toys*. New York: John Wiley and Sons, 1994. This one shows how to make a neat toy boat out of recycled materials.

Bernie Zubrowski, *Balloons*. New York: William Morrow, 1990. This book has several propulsion activities, including boats. The author also shows how to make a test trough using a piece of plastic.

GO FOR A SPIN: TOPS

OVERVIEW

Spinning things exhibit behaviors that are counter intuitive—they don't behave as one would expect. To fully understand angular momentum and gyroscopic motion, one needs a sophisticated understanding of mathematics. However, elementary and middle school kids can gain a visceral understanding of how spinning things operate that will ease their matriculation into high school physics. Just as important, kids enjoy playing with tops and will sustain the following activities for long periods of time. In these activities you empower kids to raise questions, pose answers, and conduct experiments. In other words, you get them to do science (use the scientific process) in a quest to make a better top.

SPECIAL MATERIALS NEEDED

A bicycle wheel gyroscope and a stool that spins would be great to use as demonstrations. (The physics departments at most colleges have them.) A football and a plastic plate. A pencil sharpener to sharpen the ends of the dowels.

TOOLS AND MATERIALS

Scissors (1 pair per team), one saw (for cutting dowels), stopwatches (2), drawing compasses (5), 1/4" dowels (4), masking tape (1 roll), cardboard boxes (cereal boxes or heavier cardboard), paper plates (40), launcher (see page 22), washers (1 box), and rubber bands (1 box).

LAUNCHER

Have the Inventing Guides make a launcher for the tops. Into a board (a 2 x 4 about 2' long works well) screw in one teacup hook near one end. Then screw in two other teacup hooks at the other end so they are aligned vertically, with the openings facing away from the first hook. The two hooks will retain a top while it is being spun by a rubber band which is looped over the other hook.

OPENING

Have early arrivers create games in which they use spinning washers. They could catch the spinning washers with a finger and roll them off the edge of a table to score, or catch them with two thumbs and fling them at a cup basket for two points, or they could do something much more creative. Have them demonstrate their games at the start of the lesson.

REVIEW

Invite anyone who has worked on a project at home to show it off.

DEMONSTRATION

Challenge the group to balance the plastic plate on its edge and the football on its end, and to get them to stay balanced for 5 seconds or longer. If they are unable to do it, show them that by spinning them you can get them to stay balanced. To spin the football, spin it on the floor on its side. With a robust spin, it will rise up onto one end and stay spinning for several seconds. "Why does a quarterback put spin (a spiral) on a football?" Spin gives stability.

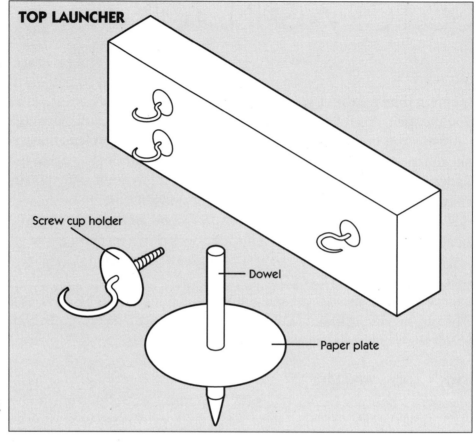

TOP LAUNCHER

Screw cup holder

Dowel

Paper plate

Then challenge participants to balance the bicycle wheel gyroscope on one handle (standing on the floor). (You can substitute a bike wheel for the bicycle wheel gyroscope; however, the effect won't be quite as good.) It won't stay balanced without spinning. Try it again, this time trying to balance it (without a spin) by placing the handle on one hand. It will fall off, unless it is spinning.

Spin makes things act weird (in counterintuitive ways). Have someone sit in the revolving stool and hold a book in each hand. Spin them slowly (did we mention to spin them slowly?) and have them pull in their arms. Repeat this several times with books of different weight. The distribution of mass effects the spin.

Finally, have someone (with long and strong arms) hold the spinning bicycle wheel gyroscope while sitting on the rotating stool. Have her or him twist the bike wheel, which will cause her or him to spin in one direction. Then have that person twist it the other direction to see what happens. Allow others to try this as time permits at the end of the session.

Ask them to describe what they have seen. Can they summarize their observations with some general statements?

READING

Hot Stuff (Microwave Oven), page 97

ACTIVITY

Have the Guides prepare both the launcher and the dowels prior to starting the activity. The dowels need to be cut into 8" lengths. The Guides can also sharpen one end of each, either in a pencil sharpener or with a file and sandpaper.

In this activity kids (working with a partner) make tops. For the first top, have them draw a circle on a piece of cardboard with a can, cut it out, and run the 8" dowel through the center. They will want to apply some tape to hold the dowel vertically against the cardboard. Then they can spin the top by hand.

After they have made their first top, invite them to try to make one that spins for a longer time. Ask them to think about what would help the top spin longer. What did they see in the demonstration that might keep a top spinning (using weights)?

Demonstrate how to use the top launcher so they can have a uniform way to spin the tops, which will allow them to compare one version of their top to the next (by timing each trial).

They can cut out more cardboard or use paper plates along with washers. Does a top made of several plates spin longer than a one-plate top? They can tape the washers to the tops. Where should they place the washers? Does it matter if they are off-balance? Does if matter if they are placed near the center or the edge?

Invite everyone to pick their best top for a "Spin-Off Test" at the end of the session. Examine the qualities of each top and invite discussion about their best features.

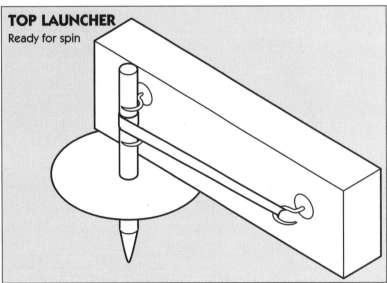

TOP LAUNCHER
Ready for spin

DEPARTURE

Suggest that participants could continue making tops at home with pencils instead of dowels and with cardboard or other recyclable materials. (If materials are in good supply, let them take their models home.) Suggest that they draw lines or solid shapes on their top and spin it to see some neat visual effects. They can report next session on what they saw. Also ask if anyone has a yoyo. A yoyo is a top that moves vertically on a string. Maybe someone could make a yoyo and bring it for the next session.

REFERENCES

Bernie Zubrowski, *Tops, Building and Experimenting with Spinning Toys*. New York: William Morrow, 1989.

ZOUNDS SOUNDS

OVERVIEW

In these activities participants will learn that sounds are vibrations. They will make sounds in several ways, and will feel, as well as hear, the sounds. You will be able to spend more time doing demonstrations as less time is required in the building activity.

TOOLS AND MATERIALS

Tin cans (disposable plastic cups can be substituted) (1 per person), string, a rag, large nails (a few), a hammer, coat hangers (cheap metal ones, one per person), straws (2 per person), scissors, a garden hose (fairly clean), spoon (large), 6 glasses, water.

OPENING

Have them fill the glasses to different levels and try to play a song by tapping on the glasses with the spoon. Each person gets two minutes to try.

From last time: did anyone bring in a project they worked on at home?

DEMONSTRATION

There are many demonstrations that convey the concepts of sound. Pick a few of these to use. You could ask each of your Inventing Guides to pick one or two demonstrations to perform. Also, rather than doing a traditional demonstration, let the participants make their own sound maker after seeing each demonstration.

D-1. Straw flutes. Take a plastic straw and chomp on one end until it is pliable. Then, with the straw between your lips, blow out to make a pleasing sound. As you do, you will feel the vibrations in your lips. This activity is easier if you trim the end of the straw so it comes to a point (like the letter V). (See Ed Sobey's book *Wrapper Rockets and Trombone Straws*, listed in the References of this activity, for a diagram.) Have each person make his or her own straw flute and try it out.

After everyone has gained experience in tooting their flute, show them how the sounds change when the length of the straw changes. While one Guide toots on a flute, cut it successively shorter with scissors, being cautious not to cut off any vital parts of the Guide.

Challenge them to make shorter or longer straws (by sticking the end of one inside the end of another straw) so a team of three or four can play different notes. Can they play a song?

When you quiet them down, ask them what made the sounds. Where did the energy come from? How did the sounds get to your ear? How did your ear collect the sounds? Would the sounds travel in space (in a vacuum)? Why were the sounds higher pitched in shorter straws? (Each straw length produces sounds of different wavelengths and we hear different wavelengths as different pitches.)

D-2. Canned tunes. Have cans prepared in advance by punching a small hole in the can (or disposable plastic cup) and passing a string through the hole. Tie a knot that won't pass through the hole on the inside of the can or cup. Cut the string at about 3' in length. Soak the string in water. Wrap a rag or paper towel around the string and slide it down the string (away from the knotted end). This makes a neat noise. Try different sizes and types of cans/cups to see which makes the best sounds.

Have the kids make their own devices and listen to each. As they rub their hands down the string, the rag sticks and then slips (much like a creaky hinge on a door) and these vibrations are carried to the can where they resonate. If you try it without the can, the sounds will be less loud. Ask the kids to hold the cans in different spots. Where does their hand dampen the sound the most/the least? Does that tell them something about how the sound is generated?

D-3. Sounds in your hose. Ask if everyone can hear you when you whisper as lightly as you can. Then ask them if they think your Ace Assistant will be able to hear you while standing in the farthest corner of the room. When they are convinced that you can't converse across the room in a whisper, prove them wrong. Stretch a hose the length of the room and talk through the hose. Invite them to try it. "Why does the hose carry sounds more effectively than just talking in the room?" (Since sounds spread, your whisper, which could barely be heard a few feet away, has stretched itself like the surface of an expanding balloon. At any point on the surface there is so little sound energy left that no one can hear you. The hose transmits the sounds without spreading so the listener gets the same sound level they would if the speaker were next to them.) Why does a doctor use a stethoscope when she listens to your heart?

D-4. Ringing in your ears. Have a volunteer hold a 3' loop of string by holding one end in each ear with their forefingers. Use the loop to hang a metal coat hanger, so it is touching nothing else except the string. Then twang the coat hanger with a spoon or fork. The volunteer will be delighted with the neat sound, while everyone else will be quite unimpressed. Have several other volunteers try it and describe the sound before you ask the question: "Why did the volunteers hear a loud sound while everyone else heard hardly anything?" (The sound reaching the volunteers' ears was carried along the string and was fuller and louder. For everyone else the sound traveled through the air and spread out before reaching their ears.)

READING

Recording Sounds (Marvin Camras), page 107

ACTIVITY

Review what they have learned about sounds: sounds are vibrations that spread in air and can be carried well in solid objects like string. You can make sounds by making something vibrate and that thing in turn vibrates air molecules, which vibrate your ear drum.

Now, invite participants to make telephones. Have them pair off and take two cans and about 10' of string. They need to make holes in the bottoms of the cans if enough weren't already made for D-2. Otherwise, they can use the same cans. They pass the string through the hole and knot the end so it rests on the inside of the can. They fix the other end of the string the same way. Then have them try talking on their phones. If they don't hear anything, have them hold the string taut. If the string pops out of the cans, have them tie the string to a nail or washer on the inside of the can. Have them feel the vibrations by gently placing a finger along the string near the tin can while they talk.

Can they add a third party to the line? How about more than three? How many can connect and still hear one another?

DEPARTURE

Ask departing participants if they can figure how many other ways there are to make noise and music. Invite them to bring in instruments they develop at home for the next session.

REFERENCES

Etta Kaner, *Sound Science*. Reading, MA: Addison-Wesley, 1991.
Ed Sobey, *Wrapper Rockets and Trombone Straws: Science at Every Meal*. New York: McGraw-Hill, 1997.

BOARD GAMES

OVERVIEW
Participants use their creativity to invent board games. They learn the difference between mock-ups and prototypes.

OPENING
As kids come in, challenge them to invent a game to be played by two people. They can use washers, pencils, and a piece of paper. They have only a few minutes to make their game, so they should start with just one or two ideas, try playing the game, and decide on changes or additions to the rules as they play. When it is time to start the lesson, invite each team to describe their game. Tell them that they just created a mock-up of a game. Mock-ups are made and changed quickly to incorporate new ideas as they arise. Once everyone agrees that the mock-up is as good as it can be, they make a prototype, which will look like the anticipated commercially made product.

REVIEW
Check to see if anyone has worked on any projects at home.

TOOLS AND MATERIALS
Paper, pencils, washers (1 box), marking pens or crayons, newsprint, cardboard and masking tape. Several board games to show. A straightedge would be helpful too.

DEMONSTRATION
Show the elements of all the games you have collected. Point out how each game incorporates the element of chance (a spinner, dice, cards to draw). Also show the markers used to keep track of progress and talk about what the board itself is supposed to represent. What other components are there? Look for an indication of the intended age range for players.

READING

Building a Monopoly on Board Games (Monopoly®), page 87

ACTIVITY

The challenge is for each team (up to four kids) to create (using brainstorming) a board game using only the simplest of materials. They should use about half the time to make mock-ups (quick and sloppy versions of the game) and test them. The remaining time should be used to create a finished prototype (a game that looks as close to the anticipated final product as possible). The mock-up phase is when ideas are suggested and tried. The prototype phase is when the selected ideas are manifested in a game.

Teams should consider:
1. What is the overarching goal of the game?
2. What will their board have on it?
3. How will they mark places on the board?
4. How will they determine the winner?
5. How will they keep track of who is winning?
6. How will they incorporate the element of chance?
7. How much skill do they want to rely on?
8. Who will play the game? (adults, kids, everyone)
9. How much will their game cost? (The retail cost is about five times the cost of production.)

They should address these questions as they are brainstorming. When they present their game to their peers at the end of the session, they need to answer these questions for everyone.

DEPARTURE

Encourage participants to keep improving their games and have them play their games with friends and family. If they have a game everyone likes, they might consider trying to sell it.

REFERENCE

Richard Levy, *Inside Santa's Workshop*. New York: Henry Holt, 1990. This book gives a good description of the toy and game industry and provides the history of some well-known games.

RACEWAYS

OVERVIEW

Kids will enjoy making gravity launchers (raceways) and testing them. They will develop an intuitive feeling for potential and kinetic energy. They will make raceways to see which design can propel a golf ball the farthest. They will make graphs of the results of their tests and use the graphs to hit targets. They will use the same launchers in the following lesson (Collisions).

TOOLS AND MATERIALS

Cardboard (several large boxes and cereal boxes), duct tape (2 rolls), golf balls (12), measuring tapes or meter sticks (3 or more), a basketball. Graph paper and pencils. Targets (flat pieces of cardboard 8" in diameter to use in the main activity) (1 target per team), Ping-Pong balls (5).

OPENING

Have them make a game of knocking down paper targets with a Ping-Pong™ ball released at the top of a short ramp. First, they have to make a ramp (made of cereal box cardboard) to hold and direct the ball, and then they need to fold paper into targets (so they stand up) and assign values to them. You might have one of the Guides build a model launcher (ramp) for them to see.

REVIEW

Did anyone work on a prior project at home? Can they show it to the group?

DEMONSTRATION

Do a series of tests to see how far the basketball will rebound when you drop it from different heights. Have one of the Inventing Guides draw a giant graph on newsprint that is taped to the wall. Have him or her mark both axes in units of feet from zero up to 8'. Also have him or her label the horizontal axis the "Drop Height" and the vertical axis the "Rebound Height."

Drop the ball from about waist high, having measured the height and calling it out to the graphing Guide. Then, with the help of another Guide, measure the rebound height. Have the graphing Guide make a large mark on the graph indicating the data point. Ask the group what they expect to happen when you drop the ball from a higher position. Then repeat the experiment, measuring both the drop and rebound heights and plotting the data on the graph. Repeat this for several more heights. Ask the graphing guide to lightly sketch in a line connecting the data points. Then ask students: If you wanted to get the ball to rebound to a height midway between the heights of two data points (show them on the graph what height you are trying to achieve), how high would you release the ball? Try the experiment and see how close you come to the desired rebound height. Tell them that graphs can be useful to predict events when you don't know for sure what will happen.

READING

Where Does It Hurt? (Band-Aids®), page 120

ACTIVITY

The challenge is to create gravity-powered launchers that will launch a golf ball the farthest distance from the launcher. The restrictions are time, materials, and height: the highest release point is 6' above the ground. Teams of three or four kids should work on each launcher. They should think, before building, of the angles they want on the down-slope and the upslope of the launcher. They should plan on conducting some tests to compare different options. And, they need to use their time wisely.

Allow them time up to 45 minutes before closing. At this time have each team demonstrate its launcher. An Inventing Guide will place a golf ball in the launcher and release it, while other Guides measure the travel distance and record it.

After each team has demonstrated their launcher, ask each team to conduct an experiment: How far will the ball go when it is launched from 5', 4', or even 3'? As they are collecting this data, have the Guides help them make a graph of their results (height of the launching position on the horizontal axis and the distance launched on the vertical axis).

See if participants can use the graph to predict how high they will have to place the ball to hit a target 3' away. Does the graph help them figure out where to launch from? Have a Guide place a target 3' away and have them try (with only one attempt—they can't learn from experience, they have to use the graph) to hit it.

DEPARTURE

Tell participants that raceways like the ones they just made could be models for roller coasters at a theme park. Suggest that they may want to draw or build some model roller coasters for a ball to travel. If they do draw or make some, have them bring them in to the next session.

REFERENCES

Bernie Zubrowski, *Raceways*. New York: William Morrow, 1985.

COLLISIONS

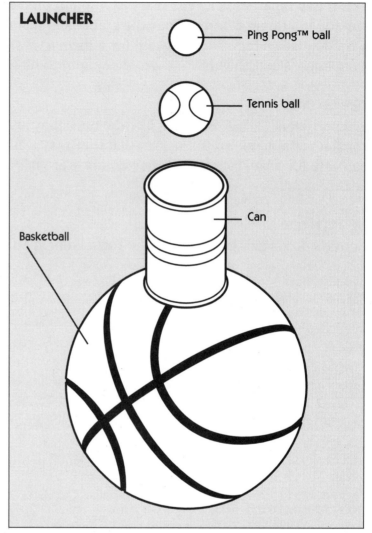

LAUNCHER

Ping Pong™ ball

Tennis ball

Can

Basketball

OVERVIEW

Using the launchers made in the previous session, kids can conduct several experiments including substituting Ping-Pong™ balls for golf balls to see how far each carries. They can also use the raceways to compare how much energy is lost in collisions between balls.

TOOLS AND MATERIALS

Demonstrations: a Newton's cradle, a basketball, tin can, and other balls to fit inside the can. Ping-Pong balls (6), other balls like racquetballs (6). The launchers (raceways) from the previous session and tape measures or meter sticks (3 or more). Duct tape. Dowels or rulers.

OPENING

Have the early arrivers create a game of pool using the rulers (or dowels) and Ping-Pong balls. See if they can use a cue ball to knock another ball into a target.

REVIEW

See if anyone has worked on projects at home.

DEMONSTRATION

If you have a Newton's cradle, demonstrate it by asking questions before releasing balls. For example: "What will happen when I release one ball?" "What will happen when I release two balls?" "What will happen when I release three balls?" "What will happen when I release one ball and release a second ball half a second later?"

Ask participants where the energy is coming from (from the sun, since you got your energy from food and you raised the ball back giving it energy of position). What happens to that energy? (It is transferred from one ball to the next. Friction in the string and wind stress [drag] reduce the speed of the balls, reducing their energy of movement.)

Show students the basketball and drop it on the floor. Have one person measure the heights of the release point and the rebound point. You might have a Guide tape a piece of newsprint to the wall to record the data. Repeat the drop experiment with a golf ball and other balls that you have. Then tape the tin can (both lids removed) onto the basketball and put one ball inside. Ask them what is going to happen. Drop the basketball—being careful that the can is pointing straight up and that there is nothing above you that will break. Or go outside to do this. Repeat this experiment, making sure that you drop the basketball from the same height you did earlier. Measure how far the basketball rebounds when it is launching the other ball.

Repeat this procedure with two balls in the tin can. Check out how high the middle ball flies compared to how high it went without another ball on top of it. Measure again the rebound of the basketball.

If you released the basketball from the same height each time, you can compare the rebound heights for the basketball by itself, with one ball in the can and with two balls in the can.

Ask them to explain what happened. Where did the energy that you put into the system go? Why did the basketball rebound to a lower height when there were other balls in the can?

READING
Collisions (Percy Julian), page 91

ACTIVITY
Have the teams set up their raceways from the preceding session and test them with a golf ball. Have them remeasure how far the golf ball traveled. Then suggest that they try the activity again, this time resting a second golf ball at the bottom of the track. When they release one ball from the top of their raceway it will roll down, collide with the second ball, and launch it. The question is: How far does the second ball travel?

The difference in travel distances (between the distances of one ball rolling down and launching itself and one ball rolling down and transferring its momentum to a second ball that is launched) indicates how much energy is lost in the collision of the two balls. Was there a lot of energy lost, or a little? They can measure the travel distances and express them as a percentage: "In the collision the launched ball traveled only 35 percent of the distance of the launched ball that didn't experience a collision."

What would happen if they replaced the second golf ball with a Ping-Pong ball? Or if they replaced the starting ball with a Ping-Pong ball? Are there other balls to test?

Where did the energy go? If you took a hundred golf balls and put them in a big container and shook it for a long time, would the temperature of the balls increase due to the collisions? (Yes.) Could you measure a temperature increase? (Yes.)

DEPARTURE

Challenge them to invent a new type of Newton's cradle, a momentum transfer machine. Could they make one using golf balls? Could they make one that lofts a Ping-Pong ball when hit by a golf ball? Invite them to bring in their creations at the next session.

REFERENCES

B. A. P. Taylor, J. Poth, and D. J. Portman, *Teaching Physics with Toys*. New York: McGraw-Hill, 1995.

FLING A FLIER

OVERVIEW

There is a set of strange objects that spin to fly. Included in this set are boomerangs, flying disks (such as Frisbees®), X-zylos®, and model helicopters. This activity focuses on the first two and helps kids make boomerangs and Frisbees out of cardboard. In the process of making and flinging spinning flyers, kids develop an understanding for gyroscopic effects.

It isn't obvious why these devices follow their trajectories, but kids can develop a feel for the physics involved. This lesson should follow the one on tops since the tops lesson exposes kids to gyroscopic motion.

TOOLS AND MATERIALS

Paper, cardboard (from a cereal box or other box; lots of it), masking tape (1 roll), washers (for weight), paper plates (50), compasses for drawing (5), scissors (12), hot glue gun (1), Ping-Pong™ ball (1), flexible straws (12), Frisbees (several), and a stopwatch. If possible: a shop vac with exhaust port and hose, and a beach ball or tennis ball.

OPENING

Have paper out for kids to make airplane models. Challenge them with designing and building a model that will stay in the air longer than everyone else's. When ready to start the lesson, have a "drop off" competition in which each person drops or flings their model. Inventing Guides can record the time. Ask the group what features of each model contributed to its success.

REVIEW

Did anyone work at home on a project from a previous lesson?

DEMONSTRATION

Show the Bernoulli effect (reduced air pressure in faster-moving air) in several different ways.

D-1. Using a flexible straw with the long end in your mouth, blow hard enough to support the Ping-Pong ball on the stream of air coming out the other end. Why does the ball stay in the stream of air? While doing this, have someone lightly blow on the ball to see if it will come out of the stream. What is the force holding the ball steady?

D-2. Hold up two pieces of paper vertically, about 2" in front of your mouth. Ask the group what they expect to happen when you blow between the two strips. Will the strips move toward each other or away from each other? Then blow to show that the faster moving air has lower pressure, and that pulls the papers inward.

D-3. Hold a piece of paper horizontally level with your lips. Ask what is going to happen when you blow across the top of it. Will it bend over farther, or will it rise? It will rise because the faster-moving air has lower pressure which will pull the paper up.

D-4. If you have access to a shop vac or a vacuum cleaner that has an exhaust port, use the stream of exhaust air to support a tennis ball or beach ball. This is a larger scale D-1.

READING

The Wright Stuff (Wright Brothers), page 118

ACTIVITY

There are two building projects here: a boomerang and a flying disk. Start with the boomerang by handing out copies of the pattern on page 37. Each kid can cut out the shape and use it as a pattern for cutting out a cardboard boomerang. Once cut out, they need to lay the boomerang on a table and bend the three arms slightly upward. Then it is ready to fly. Hold it vertically by pinching one arm between the thumb and forefinger with the concave side facing toward the left (assuming you are right-handed) and fling it. It won't fly more than a few feet before returning. With a few tries, and maybe some additional bending of the arms, you will get it to come back consistently.

Once they have mastered this simple design, challenge them to come up with other shapes and designs. Ask them what happens if they apply more or less bending to the arms. What would happen if they taped washers on to each arm? How about trying the same shape but twice as big?

BOOMERANG PATTERN (ACTUAL SIZE)

Hold in right hand.
Fling.

For the flying disk, first have everyone fling a store-bought Frisbee or other flying disk. Then have them cut out a flat disk of cardboard (use the compasses or find a round object to trace with approximately a 10" diameter) and try flinging that. The disk will turn to one side as it flies. "Does it turn to the same side if you fling it with the other hand?" The trick in designing flying disks is to get them to fly level at different throwing speeds. Compare the different commercial flying disks to see which ones fly best at slow and fast speeds. See what designs they use to keep flight level.

Teams of two can work on this project together. They should experiment to make the best flying disk. They can use cardboard circles, paper plates, an inverted paper plate, weights (washers), fins, or whatever else they can think of. They might try to mimic the leading edges and lips of the commercial products. Ask them to make notes of each trial they make, including what they learned.

With 20 minutes left in the session, hold a "fling off." Have each team demonstrate their design and describe what they found in their experiments.

DEPARTURE

Challenge them to keep working on their boomerang and flying disk designs and to bring in their improved models next time.

REFERENCES

John Kaufmann, *Fly It!* New York: Doubleday, 1980.

Benjamin Ruhe, *Many Happy Returns*. New York: Viking Press, 1977.

Benjamin Ruhe and Eric Darnell, *Boomerang*. New York: Workman, 1985.

Jearl Walker, "The Amateur Scientist: Boomerangs! How to Make Them and Also How They Fly," *Scientific American*, March 1979.

Jearl Walker, "The Amateur Scientist: More on Boomerangs, Including Their Connection with the Dimpled Golf Ball," *Scientific American*, April 1980.

STRAW BRIDGES

OVERVIEW
Kids will enjoy making bridges out of straws. The challenge is to make a bridge as long as possible that will support the weight of one golf ball hung in the middle.

TOOLS AND MATERIALS
Straws (500), masking tape (1 roll), a measuring tape or ruler, golf balls (12), paper clips (2 boxes), straight pins (12).

OPENING
Have kids pick up copies of the handout on page 41 (Chasm) and design a bridge that will enable the car to drive across. Suggest that, before they start designing, they think of bridges that they have seen. Let them have additional copies of Chasm if they have completed one design. When they are ready to start building, review the designs looking for structural elements.

REVIEW
Did anyone work at home on projects from a previous lesson?

DEMONSTRATION
Show several ways to connect straws: by jamming the end of one straw into the end of another; by jamming a partially opened paper clip in the ends of two straws; or by pinning straws together with straight pins.

Make a square using four straws attached at the corners with pins. Let them see how flimsy it is: the slightest push will collapse it. Ask how they could stop it from collapsing. One way is to brace it with cross members, forming triangles. How many different ways could there be to make triangles? (Lots, depending on the placement of the cross pieces.) Remark that triangles make structures stronger, and that kids might look for triangles in buildings and bridges.

READING

Straw Bridges to the Future (Drinking Straws), page 109

ACTIVITY

Teams of two or more kids design and build a bridge that will support a golf ball. When a bridge is ready for testing, an Inventing Guide will attach the ball in the center of the bridge. Guides will make a system for attaching the ball. (An easy way to do this is to tape a golf ball to a paper clip and use one end of the paper clip to loop onto the straw bridge.)

The challenge is to build the bridge as long as possible and still be able to support the ball. They can create the chasm by moving two desks or tables about 2' apart. Constraints are the amount of time available and 2' of masking tape per bridge. They may use as many straws as they want (up to the number available).

Before a team can start building, they must show a design sketch of their bridge to one of the Guides. The Guides don't approve the design, but do check to make sure that the team has thought through the problem and that they (not just one member) are committed to the design.

While they are building their bridges, teams may request Guides to conduct an in-progress test by hanging the golf ball. With 20 minutes left, call a halt to the building and start the official testing. Guides hang the ball as close to the exact center of the bridge as possible. When the bridge has held the weight for ten seconds, another Guide can measure the open span (what counts is not the length of the bridge, but the span that it bridges).

After all the teams have tested their bridges, have them review the best features of each bridge. What made the better bridges work? What was a good idea but for some reason failed?

DEPARTURE

Suggest that teams take their bridges apart and take them home to try building a better bridge. They should test their homemade bridges and report on their success at the next session.

REFERENCES

Bernie Zubrowski's *Drinking Straw Construction.* Boston: Little, Brown, 1981. This book contains several activities for kids using these same materials. You might also check out an encyclopedia for pictures of different types of bridges.

CHASM

ROCKETS

OVERVIEW

Kids learn about air pressure and experiment with balloon and straw rockets.

TOOLS AND MATERIALS

Balloons (50), masking tape (1 roll), empty milk cartons (half-gallon size, 2), strong string or monofilament, straws (1 box), toilet plungers (2), scissors (3), small rubber bands (24), paper (8.5" x 11" sheets), large-diameter straws (24), straightedges (rulers) (5), pencils (10, sharpened). Safety goggles (6 or more). Optional: bottle rocket launcher.

OPENING

Issue each child a balloon as he or she enters. Stress that they need to use it later and so they can't break it or lose it. Challenge them to make a rocket out of their balloon and a straw (or piece of straw). They can use rubber bands to seal the opening of their balloon against the straw(s). Does the balloon rocket work best with or without a straw, with a long straw or short straw, or with two straws? As you begin the lesson, ask who was most successful in getting his or her rocket to go far. Talk about the design characteristics.

REVIEW

Did anyone work on the project from the last lesson?

DEMONSTRATION

D-1. Stick the two plungers together, face-to-face, forming a bond. Invite the two smallest kids to pull them apart. As they struggle with them, ask everyone what is holding the plungers together. Someone will say a vacuum is holding them, but a better way to think

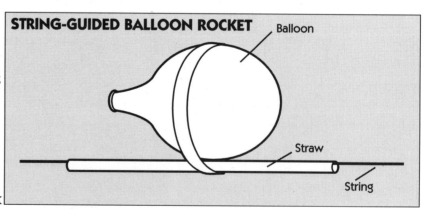

STRING-GUIDED BALLOON ROCKET — Balloon, Straw, String

about it is that the air pressure from the surrounding air is squeezing them together.

D-2. If you have access to a bottle rocket launcher and have space outdoors, do one or two launches. Ask what is propelling the rocket upward. Where did the energy come from to launch the rocket? (The sun, food you ate.) If the pump has a gauge, tell them what the pressure is. When a bottle lands, examine the inside to see a cloud that formed when the pressure was released.

D-3. Take a gallon (milk) container and pour very hot water inside. Slosh the water around with the lid on, and then dump it out. Replace the lid and hold the container in very cold water. While waiting for the air inside to cool, ask participants what is happening. What has happened to the air pressure inside the container? (It dropped as the air temperature dropped.) Did the surrounding air pressure change? (No.) So now you have more air pressure outside the container than inside. What do you expect to happen when there is a large pressure difference?

Try this experiment in reverse. Start with cold water in the jug and swish it around. Then run hot water over the capped jug. Now what do they expect to happen? Stand back. In some cases you may need to pry up one side of the lid to get it to take off. Suggest that everyone try these at home and use ice water for the cold water. Talk about how hot water increases the pressure by making the molecules more active and cold water decreases the pressure by making the molecules less active.

D-4. Have two Guides blow up balloons, one fairly full and the other one much less so. Connect one to a straw by using masking tape or a rubber band and keep the neck pinched (the balloons, not the Guides) to keep air inside. Now connect the other balloon to the other end of the straw and keep its neck pinched. Ask what is going to happen when you release the necks allowing air to flow from one balloon to the other. Will air flow to equalize the size of the balloons? Release the two and wait for the surprise. (The fuller balloon will get bigger at the expense of the smaller one.) The air pressure in the fuller balloon was less than in the smaller one, and air flowed from the small one to the big one. But they knew that. Ask them at what point is it hardest to blow up a balloon and at what point is it easiest. Hardest is just after you start to fill the balloon. Easiest is at the end (just before it breaks). (If you want to know the gory details, see Jearl Walker's article listed in the References for this activity.)

READING
Blast Off (Robert Goddard), page 84

ACTIVITY
Form teams of three or four kids. There are two activities for them: making a balloon rocket and making a straw rocket. They all should contribute to both rockets.

A-1. Have the Guides set up two guide strings across the room. Use a strong string or monofilament line tied high enough so no one will walk into it. Before tying off the second end, have them string two straws onto the lines. They need to make the strings as taut as possible. (A trucker's knot or come-along knot will help.)

The challenge for the teams is to make a rocket that will reach the far side of the room, guided by the string. They can use one or more balloons, straws, and other materials that they can find. Can they figure out a way to make a two-stage rocket? Can they place rockets on two sides of the straw? Can they better control the exhaust of the balloon by using straws?

A-2. Kids make straw rockets. They use pencils as a form for making the rocket bodies. Kids cut a paper strip 1" to 2" wide and 8.5" long. They wrap it around the pencil lengthwise and tape it. They can test it to ensure that it will slide easily on and off one of the straws. Then, have them cut *V*s out of one end of the paper tube so it looks like a tiny king's crown. Insert the sharpened pencil into the paper tube to make a form so they can tape the king's crown down to a point. Now they can add fins of their own design for the other end of the tube. Before they launch their rockets, designate one area for testing them. Everyone must wear safety goggles or glasses in this area. When ready, have participants slide their rocket onto their straw and give it a blast of air.

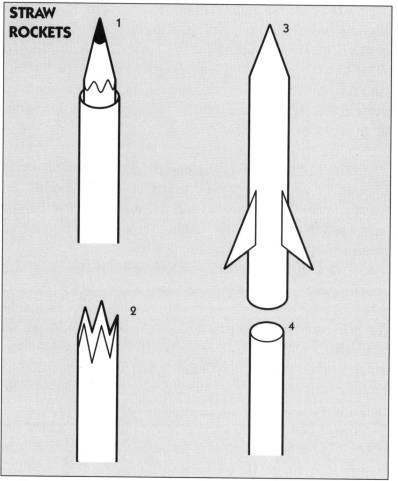

STRAW ROCKETS

At the end of the lesson, have a blast off for distance across the room.

DEPARTURE

You might encourage kids to examine the bottle rocket launcher so they can make their own, and encourage them to try balloon rockets on a string. If they live in an apartment building, they could hang the string vertically with the bottom weighted with a rock or trash can, and see how high they can get their rocket to fly.

REFERENCES

Jearl Walker, "The Amateur Scientist," *Scientific American*, December 1989. (Why are the first few puffs the hardest when you blow up a balloon?)

GET A CHARGE OUT OF THIS

OVERVIEW

Kids discover the basics of DC electrical circuits and see demonstrations of static electricity. They discover that some materials conduct electricity well and that others don't, that circuits need to be complete or closed to work, that switches let you open and close a circuit, and that series and parallel circuits do different things.

TOOLS AND MATERIALS

Circuit boards (see References), wire, flashlight bulbs (40), batteries (40), electric motors (12, these are inexpensive DC motors), balloons (12), string, meter stick, salt and pepper, paper and pencils. For conductivity test: plastic, paper, wood, nails, a belt.

OPENING

Have kids work in teams of two or three to brainstorm all the things they use that run on electricity. Have them designate the source of electricity by marking each item with DC for battery powered or AC for electricity that is accessed from a floor or wall plug. Review the lists when everyone has arrived.

REVIEW

Did anyone make progress on the project from the last lesson?

DEMONSTRATION

Using an inflated balloon, demonstrate how accumulated charges provide an attractive force. Prepare for these demonstrations by running through them before class so you know what will be attracted to the charged balloon. You may need to start with new balloons for each demonstration if you can't remove their charge.

D-1. Show that an inflated balloon won't stick to a wall or ceiling. Then rub it on clothing or your hair and show that it will stick to the wall. "What is causing it to stick when gravity is pulling it down?"

D-2. Show how an inflated balloon won't pick up salt or pepper spread on a piece of paper until it has been charged. Let everyone see the salt and pepper and, if possible, let them crowd around to see the salt and pepper jump up to attach itself to the charged balloon.

D-3. Hang two inflated but uncharged balloons by strings two feet below a supporting meter stick. Tie them so they rest about 1" from each other. Then charge each balloon by rubbing the sides closest to each other on your clothing and then release them to hang again.

D-4. Using a volunteer with long hair, see if you can pick up some hair with a charged balloon.

In each demonstration you can ask, "What did rubbing the balloon do?" (It transferred charges between the balloon and clothing. Since the balloon doesn't conduct charge, the charges can't migrate—they are stuck there. That's why we call this static electricity—it doesn't move.) "In the circuits you are about to build, the charges can move because we use conductors, wire." Pop the balloons and hold them for later use to test the conducting abilities of balloons.

READING:

Before the Bulb (Thomas Alva Edison), page 83

ACTIVITY

Have someone identify and name all the components on the circuit boards. Then ask what is required to make one light up. (A complete circuit is required so electricity can travel from the battery to the light and back to the battery.)

Have each team of two or three make a circuit to light one bulb. "What happens if you remove one wire? What happens if you remove the other wire (instead of the first one). Does it matter which wire you remove?" (No.)

"Wires conduct electricity to the bulb so it can light. Let's test some other materials to see which ones conduct electricity. Try the balloons, paper, and other things you can find. Do experiments in which you replace one wire with the material to be tested. Write down which materials conduct electricity and which don't." After everyone has had an opportunity to test several materials, ask them to report on what they found.

"Now, try hooking up two light bulbs. Let us know when you have two bulbs glowing." Presumably someone will hook them up parallel, giving you the chance to compare parallel and series. If not, have one of the Guides quickly hook up a spare board in parallel. "Is there a difference between the two types of circuits? Which one burns brighter?"

"Try hooking up three bulbs." Compare parallel and series again. Then try combinations of bulbs and electric motors or buzzers. See if someone can get the motor to spin at different speeds by adding or removing bulbs from the circuit.

Suggest that someone invent a switch to use. For example, they could use a nail to close a circuit making it easier to turn it on and off.

Review what they learned.

DEPARTURE

Tell them not to try these experiments unless they are sure they are using small batteries. Using the electricity from their home circuits could hurt them. "Don't experiment or play with it." However, they can build their own circuit boards at home using batteries.

REFERENCES

Ovid K. Wong, *Experimenting with Electricity and Magnetism.* New York: Franklin Watts, 1993. This has ideas for making circuit boards from inexpensive materials.

Bernie Zubrowski, *Blinkers and Buzzers: Building and Experimenting with Electricity and Magnetism.* New York: Beech Tree, 1991.

CIRCUIT BOARDS

The above references have good ideas for making circuit boards (and for other electricity projects). Here is one approach derived from them:

1. Cut a 1" x 12" pine board into foot-long sections.
2. Use brass nails (1/2" long) as contacts. For switches: nail paper clips to the boards with an exposed wire wrapped around the nail. Connect a second wire to another nail and pound it one paper clip length away. You can slide the paper clip to contact the second nail to complete a circuit.
3. You can make electric bulb holders from clothespins. Nail a clothespin to the board through the center opening in the pin's spring. Wrap exposed wire around the side connector of a bulb and hold it in place in the jaws of the clothespin. To connect the end of the bulb, wrap exposed wire around a brass nail and drive it into the board at a location where the bulb held by the clothespin will make contact.
4. Make a battery holder by rolling four D-cell batteries (all headed in the same direction) in two sheets of paper. Tape the paper tightly. Jam a small piece of aluminum foil into the paper tube to connect to the battery terminals. Poke a large nail through the tube at each end, so it touches the foil. Now wrap exposed wire around each nail.
5. Or go to Radio Shack and ask for help.

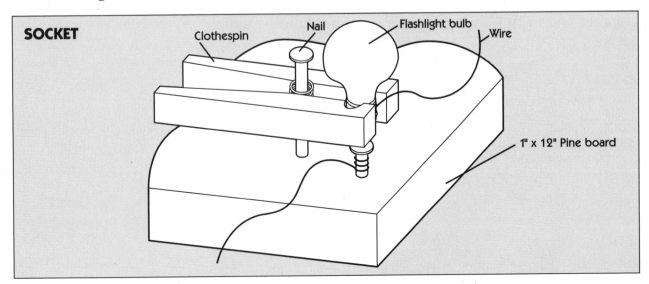

SOCKET — Clothespin — Nail — Flashlight bulb — Wire — 1" x 12" Pine board

DRATS, SCRAMBLED AGAIN!

OVERVIEW

This is a different version of an egg drop, one that calls for materials found at home so kids can replicate the experience there. Although the activity will be easy to prepare for, the demonstration will require more preparation.

MATERIALS

Scissors (6), half-gallon milk jugs (12), rubber bands (60), straws (60), string (1 ball), masking tape (1 roll), eggs (1 dozen), Slinky® (6), discarded light bulb, small paper sack, rubber ball and hammer, 6' stepladder (or a stairwell), generous wad of newspaper, a wooden slat, and a plywood slat.

OPENING

Have the Slinkys out and challenge the kids to make a staircase out of available materials so the Slinky can walk down. What else can they get the Slinky to do? When you are ready to being the lesson, ask: "What kind of machine is a Slinky?" (It's a spring.) "How do springs work?" (The more you stretch them, the greater is the force that pulls them back.) "Where do you find springs?" (In suspension systems in cars, in office chairs, staplers [inside to push the staples forward, and to rebound after you affix a staple], a paper clip is a spring, and so on.) If possible, hold up some of these examples so they can see what you mean.

REVIEW

See if anyone brought in projects worked on at home.

DEMONSTRATION

This demonstration deals with "why stuff breaks."

D-1. Start by taping a wooden slat (30" long, 1/4" thick, 1" wide pine board) onto a table so 2' extend beyond the table. To help hold the slat in place, have a Guide press down on the end supported by the table. "What happens when I press down on the free end?" (It bends.) "When I release it, what happens?" (It rebounds like a spring.) "Does it go immediately back to its starting point?" (No, it passes the neutral point, keeps going and then starts going the other direction, back and forth.) "What happens if I press it even farther?" (It rebounds farther.) "If I press too hard, what happens?" (The board can't bend any more, so it breaks.)

D-2. Repeat with a similar-sized piece of plywood. "Does it bend as far?" After you break the wood, have someone compare the slat and the plywood to see what the differences are. (Plywood consists of thin layers [veneers] of wood peeled off logs and then glued, layer on layer. Each layer is set so its grain goes a different direction, giving the plywood great strength, as opposed to having all the grain in one direction.) Reinforce the idea that things break when they can't respond to forces exerted on them by bending: they have reached the limits of their ability to bend.

D-3. Wood can bend and so it gives before breaking. How about rubber? Stretch a rubber band. Fling it across the room. The rubber band stored energy, just like a spring. But what happens when you get to the point where it can't stretch any farther? It breaks.

D-4. Take the rubber ball and drop it in the paper sack. "When I hit the ball with a hammer, it can bend, store the energy, and push back on the hammer." Whack the ball and have students watch to see the hammer rebound. Rubber gives even more than wood does. How does glass behave?

D-5. Place the lightbulb in the sack. "What is going to happen when I hit it with the hammer?" (It will break.) "Why will it break?" (Because the glass won't bend much. It will reach its limit of bending and break.) Smash the sucker. "Did the hammer rebound?" (No. Instead of storing energy and returning it like a spring, the glass shattered.) Hold up an egg and explain that although an eggshell will bend a little, like glass it will break when given a sufficient whack. Their job, in a few minutes, will be to save their egg.

READING

Bouncing Back from Adversity (Goodyear, Rubber and Bungee Jumping), page 85

ACTIVITY

Provide for each group of two or three kids the following materials: 5 rubber bands, 5 straws, and 1 half-gallon juice or milk carton. They can also use up to 2' of masking tape and 2' of string. Scissors are available. When they are ready, they can have one egg. Their challenge is to design and build a crashproof container for their egg out of the materials provided.

Step 1. Name the egg.
Step 2. Figure out how to use the straws to slow down the impact and use the rubber bands to cushion the egg.
Step 3. Make the crash container.
Step 4. Kiss your egg goodbye and test your container.

When ready at the end of the lesson, a Guide will drop each container starting at tabletop height. Crash containers with surviving eggs will go to the next round, which will be approximately 2' higher. For later rounds, have a Guide use a stepladder to get the elevation needed. Have another Guide steady the ladder by placing one foot on the support on the side opposite the one with steps, and by holding on with both hands. Before dropping any containers, make a target area (cleanup area) with newspapers.

As each team's entry is about to be dropped, announce the name of the egg and comment on its design. Ask the others if they think it will succeed or fail. Then drop away.

DEPARTURE

Tell the kids that there are many other ways to do egg drops. For example, they could make parachutes to slow the rate of descent, or they could using packing material. With adult supervision, they could try these other methods at home and report back next session on their success.

According to the 1996 edition of *The Guinness Book of Records*, the record for egg drop is 700 feet. An Englishman successfully dropped an egg from a helicopter in August 1994.

REFERENCES

The Sky's the Limit with Math and Science. Fresno, CA: AIMS Activities in Aerodynamics, 1987.

HOT SHOTS, PART X

OVERVIEW

Ballistics with rubber bands is the topic. Kids learn enough about a rubber band launcher that they can hit targets based on graphs of the trajectories. They also think about potential and kinetic energies in terms of the flight of rubber bands. Discretion is called for to prevent an eye injury. When rubber bands are being launched, the launchers must face onto the target range and anyone in the range must be wearing eye protection. Anyone shooting rubber bands deliberately at someone is excused from participating in the activity.

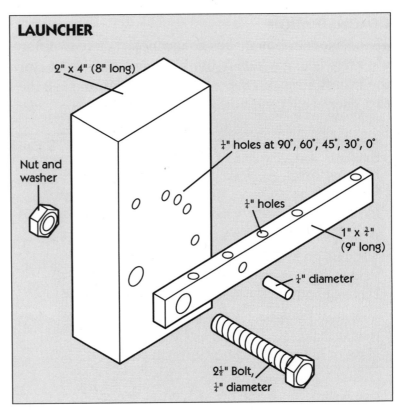

LAUNCHER

2" x 4" (8" long)

Nut and washer

$\frac{1}{4}$" holes at 90°, 60°, 45°, 30°, 0°

$\frac{1}{4}$" holes

1" x $\frac{3}{4}$" (9" long)

$\frac{1}{4}$" diameter

2$\frac{1}{2}$" Bolt, $\frac{1}{4}$" diameter

TOOLS AND MATERIALS

Launchers (8), rubber bands (36), targets (cardboard circles approximately 12" in diameter) (12), scissors, paper and pencils for each team, goggles, meter sticks (8), stuff for the demonstration (see suggestion under Demonstration), graph paper, masking tape.

OPENING

As kids come in, the Inventing Guides can introduce them to the launchers and have them practice launching. The Guides can set up empty cereal boxes (maybe cut the tops to form crenulations) as castle targets for them. One Guide needs to be stationed at the range to ensure safety procedures.

At the start of the lesson, ask if those kids who launched bands had fun. "How far were you able to shoot the bands? Were you able to hit the targets? Since the bands were moving, they had energy. Where did the energy come from? Can you trace it back to the sun? Since the bands stopped (when they hit the floor), where did the energy go?" "We're going to do some more work with the ballistics launchers later."

REVIEW

Did anyone continue work at home on the project from last time?

DEMONSTRATION

This demonstration makes connections between different systems that store energy. The objective is to get kids to think in new ways about storing energy. From a bag you pull out the widest array of energy storage systems and ask the group how they access the energy (get energy out) and how energy gets in.

ENERGY STORAGE	MECHANISM OF ACCESSING ENERGY	INPUT
D.C. battery	connect to a circuit	at factory/chemical storage . . . sunlight
car battery	connect to car's circuits	alternator . . . sunlight
banana	eat	sunlight
hot dog	eat	sunlight
lighter	flick on, igniting the gas	sunlight
rubber band	releasing stretched band	stretching it . . . sunlight
holding a book up	letting go	lifting it . . . sunlight
mousetrap	wiggle the release	setting trap . . . sunlight
glass of hot water	pour through pipes, etc.	hot water heater . . . sunlight

See if they can come up with other energy storage systems.

READING

The Quest for Synthetic Rubber (Silly Putty®), page 116

ACTIVITY

Kids learn about the ballistic characteristics of their systems. They collect data systematically so they will be able to hit targets based on their data collection.

Break up into eight groups and give each group three rubber bands. Each team is to take a spot in the launching area. If possible, assign one Guide to every two teams. With one team member measuring distance, one recording and one launching, each team records and graphs the distance achieved for each energy level at one elevation. When the data have been collected and graphed (Guides available to help), team members rotate positions so everyone has the opportunity to do each activity. Then they repeat this to get data for the other elevations.

During this testing, only one team member is in the target area (the one making measurements) and that member must wear eye protection.

When the teams have collected the data, Guides place targets marked for each team in the target area. Guides should check the data for each team to ensure that they locate the targets within the range of possible landings. Once the targets are in place, one team member measures the distance to the target, and the team, consulting their graphs, decides the elevation and energy level to use to hit the target.

With sufficient time, repeat this to include short-, medium-, and long-range targets. Record 10 points for a band landing completely on the target and 5 points if partially on.

At the end of the activity, ask if the teams were able to use their graphs to help figure out the launch angle and energy level. "At what launch angle did you get the longest flight? As you increased the energy level, did it always fly farther?"

TO LAUNCH

Set the peg in one of the five holes that will lock the arm horizontally—15°, 30°, 45°, 60°, or vertically. Place two other pegs in two of the five holes on the top of the arm. Stretch the rubber band between these two pegs. To launch, pull up the peg closest to the bolt.

DEPARTURE

Caution participants to be careful with anything that springs back or flies, and to never shoot a rubber band at someone. Ask if they could design and build a different kind of launcher for rubber bands and ask them to bring it to the next class if they do. Don't have them bring it, however, if your school considers rubber-band launchers to be guns.

REFERENCES

Bob Friedhoffer, *Toying Around with Science.* New York: Franklin Watts, 1995.
Don Radford, *Science, Models, and Toys.* London: Simon & Schuster, 1974.

HOT SHOTS, PART X^2

OVERVIEW

In "Hot Shots, Part X," kids shot rubber bands and learned the optimal angle for achieving distance. In this version, teams make catapults and launch Ping-Pong balls. The goal is to get maximum distance. To build these devices, students will use hand tools. Inventing Guides can cut the wood prior to the start of the activity and supervise the construction to minimize bruises. Younger kids will need help assembling their launchers.

Although this activity comes close to the topic of guns, we try not to draw attention to guns. We use "launchers" rather than "shooters." There is lots of good physics to learn here, but we won't want to use this topic if we let discussions drift into war games or street violence.

MATERIALS

Provide the following for 12 teams of two students each: Cardboard boxes (several), scissors (6 pairs), masking tape, studs (2 x 4s) (3), 1 x 2s (16'), small hinges (12), 1.5" nails, hammers (6), rubber bands (1 box), saws (2), Ping-Pong balls (12), paper cups (12), pliers (3), and a hand drill with bits. One plastic spoon. Three eggs and a bed sheet.

OPENING

As kids come in, they can make castles out of cardboard to be targets for their launchers. They can cut boxes into long castle walls with crenulations, towers, sally ports, and a gate house. They will need to make something (a support) to keep the walls from falling over. Do they have a name for the castle? Who lives in the castle? The names of the castle and its residents should be printed on the outside walls of the castle.

REVIEW

Who worked on the rubber-band launcher at home?

DEMONSTRATION

What happens in a collision involving a raw egg? Have two Guides hold a bed sheet length-wise. They should roll up the bottom of the sheet and hold it in their lowered hands to catch and retain tossed eggs. Have the most accurate thrower toss a raw egg at the center of the sheet; it won't break. Repeat this for the doubting Thomases and then take the last egg and break it open to show that it wasn't hard-boiled.

To accelerate a few heartbeats, slip a table tennis ball into the container of eggs and toss it into the audience after you have shown them that the eggs are raw.

READING

From Castles to Kevlar®, page 94

ACTIVITY

Preparation: Guides should have the following pieces of wood cut prior to the start of the activity: 12 2' lengths of the studs and 24 1' lengths of 1 x 2s. Have them also set up the castle at the end of the room, giving lots of room for teams to launch table-tennis balls when they are ready.

Each team of two to four kids receives one piece of 2 x 4, two pieces of 1 x 2, 1 hinge, 1 paper cup (to hold the ball for launching) and several rubber bands. They can request additional pieces of 1 x 2, nails, and masking tape, and can ask to use the hammer (with supervision). Before they start assembling their catapult, they need to sketch it out and show it to a Guide. When a Guide has seen that they have a plan, he or she can authorize the team to use a hammer.

Teams can try different arrangements of parts to achieve maximum range but need to be finished 30 minutes before closing time.

Testing of the catapults can start at a modest range: teams must hit the castle walls or fly over the castle wall without bouncing. Teams can try three shots to qualify for succeeding rounds. After all teams have completed the first round, Guides can set the launch position back for each succeeding round. As the "launch off" continues, ask the group what features of the design seem to be responsible for success, and what improvements could be made to a design.

DEPARTURE

Ask the Guides to stick around to disassemble the catapults so the parts can be used again.

Suggest that kids try using plastic spoons at home to make launchers for paper balls. Challenge them to see how far they can get a plastic spoon launcher to work, and to bring in a sketch of their device for the next lesson.

REFERENCES

David Macaulay, *Castle*. Boston: Houghton Mifflin, 1977.

SORTED AFFAIRS

OVERVIEW

Sorting coins or washers of different sizes challenges teams to be creative. They need to design a system to get coins into a sizing mechanism, get them sorted without getting stuck, and deposit them in different containers.

TOOLS AND MATERIALS

Cardboard (several boxes for each team), masking tape (2 rolls), scissors, toilet paper and paper towel tubes, dowels (helpful, but not necessary), metal washers of four different sizes (or use coins: penny, nickel, dime, and quarter), pencils (1 per person), 1 stopwatch.

OPENING

Challenge kids to invent a game they can play on a table using only washers—different from the spinning game invented previously. Have them play the game and develop the rules. When reporting on their game to the group, ask them first to explain what the objective of the game is and then how it is played.

REVIEW

Check to see if anyone worked at home on a previous project.

DEMONSTRATION

Coin rubbings. Show how you can determine the denomination of a coin that is under a piece of paper without lifting the paper. Slide the side of a pencil lead or crayon across the surface to reveal the image of the coin. Have the group try it with coins or other objects that have raised surfaces.

READING
New Money (Credit Cards), page 100

ACTIVITY
Teams of three or four kids work together to design and build devices that will sort a handful of coins (or washers) into four containers. The teams need to think about how they want to meet the challenge, draw a sketch of their solution, build it, and test it. When they show a Guide that they have a sketch of their ideas, they can begin to build.

They can roll the coins down a sorting chute or place them on a vibrating tray (vibrations to come from one of the team members) or try some other mechanism.

Evaluation of designs comes at the end of the lesson. Each team is handed the same number and same variety of coins to sort. They are timed to see how quickly their mechanism works. For each missorted coin (or coin that hangs up in the mechanism and requires human intervention to remove it), add 5 seconds to a team's time. The design with the fastest adjusted time is deemed the optimal design.

DEPARTURE
Suggest that kids try the coin rubbing at home. They could rub: manhole covers (watch for traffic), geographic survey markers, bricks. . . . Also suggest that since many banks no longer count and sort change, there is a market for an inexpensive coin sorter for small businesses. Maybe someone can improve upon their design and make a prototype for testing in a store.

REFERENCES
David Macauley, *The Way Things Work*. Boston: Houghton Mifflin, 1988.

ELECTROMAGNETS

OVERVIEW

Kids work in groups of three or four to design and build electromagnetic cranes. The challenge is to pick up as many nails as they can with three lifts of their crane. They have to deposit the nails into a cup.

TOOLS AND MATERIALS

Magnet wire (25' per team), batteries (4 D cells per team), paper (6 sheets of 8.5" x 11"), masking tape (1 roll), aluminum foil (1 roll), rubber bands, nails (1 large box of 2"-long nails), string (1 ball), cardboard boxes (1 per team), magnets, large nails (1 per team), paper cups (1 per team), steel balls, and dowels (1/4", 1 per team), saw to cut the dowels.

OPENING

Challenge participants to devise a game in which the object is to push a steel ball into a goal using the magnets you provide.

REVIEW

Check to see if anyone has made progress on previous projects.

DEMONSTRATION

Guides demonstrate how to make a direct-current motor powered by a battery. They should try this before the day of the lesson to ensure they can get it to work.

Step 1. Forming the field coil. Rubber-band four pencils together to use as a form for making a coil. Wind the "magnet wire" (available from Radio Shack) around the pencils ten times. Leave two inches of wire at each end of the coil. Scrape the insulation off the top surface only of each lead wire.

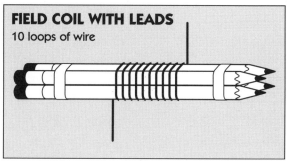

FIELD COIL WITH LEADS
10 loops of wire

Then bend a hook into each end so it won't fall out of its support.

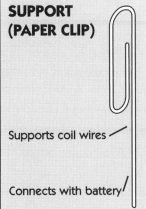

Step 2. Make supports. Straighten the long end of two paper clips leaving an elongated loop at one end and a straight piece of wire at the other.

Step 3. Attach the largest disk-shaped magnet you can find to one side of the D-cell battery. Use either glue or a rubber band to hold it in place.

Step 4. Attach each paper clip support to one end of the battery and hold it in place with rubber bands and/or tape. The ends of the clips have to be touching the battery contacts. Position them so they are standing up above the side of the battery that the magnet is on.

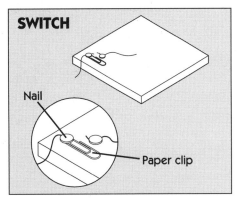

Step 5. Position the field coil directly above the magnet by resting each end of the wire leads in one of the paper clip loops.

Step 6. Give the loop a push. It should keep going. If not, increase the battery power available by connecting several batteries in a series. If it still doesn't go, get a bigger magnet. This demonstration takes some work, but it is really fun to see.

Explain what's happening. You have made a direct-current motor. The loop coil is an electromagnet that is turned on only when one side of the wire leads is in contact with the paper-clip supports. When the electromagnet is on, one side will be drawn toward the fixed magnet and the other side will be repelled. When the electromagnet is facing the other direction, there is no force moving it, but its momentum will keep it turning.

READING
The Battle of the Currents (AC *vs.* DC), page 112

ACTIVITY

Teams of three or four kids are to make electromagnetic cranes to lift as many nails as they can from a pile and deposit them in a cup. Each team gets 25' of magnet wire and can experiment to see how much provides the optimum lift.

They form the electromagnets by winding the magnet wire around the large nail. They need to leave enough wire at each end to provide leads to the battery case.

If they haven't made them previously, they can now make a battery case. Taking six sheets of paper (8.5" x 11"), they roll four batteries together so that the batteries are in a straight line and each battery is touching the opposite end of the batteries ahead and behind it. They wrap this tightly and tape it in place. Next they jam a 2" square of aluminum foil into each end of the case, making sure each is in contact with the battery terminals. Then they poke a nail through the rolled paper so it contacts the aluminum foil. They can use the protruding nails as contacts to draw electric power.

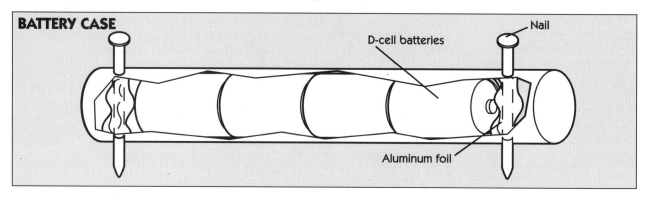

BATTERY CASE

Nail

D-cell batteries

Aluminum foil

While one pair of kids is working on their electromagnet, the other pair can be building the crane. They can use dowels for support and the string to tie to the large nail in the electromagnet. By pulling on the string they can raise and lower the electromagnet. They can use the cardboard boxes as a base for their cranes.

Toward the end of the lesson, have each team demonstrate their device. Each should get three lifts to pick up as many nails as possible. During the demonstration, no one from a team can touch any nails. (They can maneuver the cup to catch the nails and maneuver the box/crane to get to the nails and cup, but they can't touch the nails.) When finished, have them count the number of nails in the cup. Find out how many turns of wire each team used and what other differences there were between different designs.

DEPARTURE

Challenge kids to figure out where there are electromagnets in their home. Every device that uses electricity is a candidate. Those devices that make something move or make sounds or pictures all use electromagnets. Ask them to bring in a list of machines they found in their homes that used electromagnets.

REFERENCES

Robert Carrow, *Put a Fan in Your Hat!* New York: McGraw-Hill, 1997. Use this for advanced projects.

Robert Ehrlich, *Turning the World Inside Out.* Princeton, NJ: Princeton Paperbacks, 1990. This is the reference for making the demonstration motor. It is packed with great demos.

Bernie Zubrowski, *Blinkers and Buzzers.* New York: Beech Tree, 1991.

RUBBER-BAND CARS

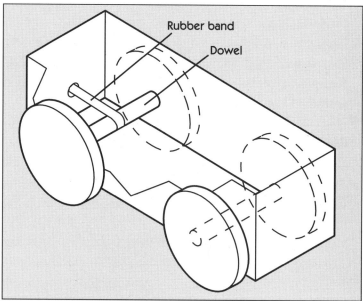

OVERVIEW

Teams of two or three kids design and make model cars powered by rubber bands.

TOOLS AND MATERIALS

Wheels (4 per team) (2 1/2" diameter, cut from 3/8" plywood with a circle saw), 1/4" dowels—6" long—for axles (2), half-gallon milk containers (1 per team), tape, rubber bands, scissors, paper clips, large-diameter straws (1 box), string, masking tape, hot glue gun, paper and pencils. Demonstration: large metal coffee can, large bolt with several nuts, 2 toothpicks, and a twist tie.

OPENING

Ask early arrivers to design (draw) cars that don't use four wheels. They can draw their designs on paper and show them to the group.

REVIEW

Check to see if anyone has been working on projects at home.

DEMONSTRATION

Have one of the Guides build a roll-back toy prior to the lesson. To do so, the Guide needs a metal coffee can, rubber bands, a large bolt with several nuts, two nails, and a twist tie. Punch a hole in the end of the can and squeeze a loop of the rubber band through it. Keep the rubber band from slipping back through by running a nail through the loop. Pull the rubber band tight from the inside of the can. Screw the nuts onto the bolt and, using the twist tie, attach them to the loop of the rubber band. Now, make a hole in the removable lid and run a loop of the rubber band through it and secure it in place with another nail. Snap the lid on, and it is ready for testing. Use a piece of tape to keep the nails from sliding on the lids.

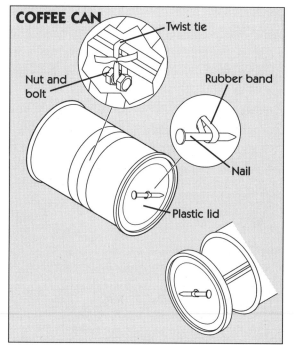

To wind up the toy, roll it in one direction along the floor. With sufficient winding it should be ready to release in the other direction.

For the demonstration, have the toy wound up prior to starting. Then show the "magic can" that will roll back when the Guide rolls it away. (Make sure you are rolling it in the right direction, otherwise it will keep on rolling away from you). Ask the kids what made the can roll back. After they have given some ideas, open it up to reveal the rubber band motor.

READING

The Most Popular Four-Wheel Vehicle (Shopping Carts), page 114

ACTIVITY

Each team selects its milk container and up to four wheels. (They can use fewer wheels if they want, or can trade another team to get one of their wheels.) The challenges are to get the axles inserted parallel to each other and with a minimum of friction; to figure out how to attach the rubber band to power the car; and to figure out how to have the car roll as far as possible after the rubber band has gotten it accelerated. They can use other materials as they find them.

They should first concentrate on getting their car to move as far as possible with little or no resistance. They can make an incline to test their model. Only after they have convinced themselves that their car rolls easily should they start making the rubber-band motor.

As a first effort they might attach the rubber band to one axle and the body of the car. However, they will soon discover that this design will cause the car to stop rather than continuing to roll with its built-up momentum. They need to think about how to have the car continue to roll after the rubber band has released its stored energy.

At the end of the lesson, examine the designs and ask the kids to predict which ones will work well and on what they are basing their predictions. Then invite each team to demonstrate how far their car can travel under the power of one rubber band.

DEPARTURE

Invite the teams to make better car models at home (but to leave these models here so the wheels and axles can be used again). They can make wheels out of jar lids, thread spools, or wood. Challenge them to bring in their homemade models at the next session.

REFERENCES

Barbara Eichelberger and Connie Larson, *Construction for Children.* Menlo Park, CA: Dale Seymour Publications, 1993. This book has several rubber-band-powered projects for kids.

SECURE CODES

SECRET CODES

OVERVIEW

Teams devise a code and a system of communication to get a message from one member of their team to another. Nominally this activity is about communication, but it taxes participants' powers of logic and creativity.

TOOLS AND MATERIALS

An assortment of stuff: paper, markers, dowels, cardboard, scissors, masking tape, cans, and whatever else you can pull together.

OPENING

Challenge kids to communicate some simple ideas to one another. Have kids work in pairs. One draws three triangles on a piece of paper and doesn't show the partner. The challenge is to tell the partner how to replicate the drawing without either person looking at the other person's paper and without the person trying to replicate the drawing asking any questions. Have each pair of students compare their drawings to see if they have come close.

REVIEW

Ask if anyone has been working on projects at home.

READING

How Telecommunications Got Started (Samuel Morse), page 98

DEMONSTRATION

Note that the order has been changed to take advantage of Morse Code. For this demonstration, have Guides encode a simple message in Morse Code and give it to the group by raising hands (right hand for dot, left for dash). Start with a single letter, and then, as the kids get proficient, encode words and phrases.

ACTIVITY

A-1. The challenge is to get a simple sentence communicated across the room without using voice, printed messages, or drawings. Teams have ten minutes to devise a code that will allow them to converse using the following words:

NOUNS	VERBS	DESCRIPTORS
Bill	bring	quickly
Sally	take	red
book	write	blue
name	read	carefully
toy	play	now

After the teams have devised their communications strategy, have them split into two squads: sending and receiving. The two team halves are to stand at least 10' away, and farther would be better.

Give the sending team a sample sentence to try: "Bill bring red book."
When all the teams have mastered this, have them try more complex sentences, such as:
"Sally write (in) book and read to Bill."
"Carefully play (with the) toy."
"(What is the) name of toy?"

After they have tried the question, they may devise additional codes to allow them to use past tense or future tense as well as asking questions. Try a few more sentences.

A-2. Now they can write messages to one another using letters, symbols, or numbers, but the challenge will be for only their team to be able to read the messages. Each team devises a code. They can make a copy of it for each half of their team. When they have made a code, give each team a different but equally difficult sentence to encode. Everyone should know that the messages will use pronouns (I, we, she, us, he, they) but no proper nouns. The messages will all contain at least one two-letter word from this list: *of, in, on, am.* The encoding half of each team writes their encoded message on a piece of paper and posts it on a wall for all to see. Then they can try to decode the other teams' messages while the receiving half of the teams decode their own team's message.

The encoding and decoding squads of each team can't talk to each other; and it would be best to keep the decoding squads beside their own team's message and the encoding squads free to wander to all the other teams' messages.

Teams score points for every word of their own message that they decode (5 points) and every word of another team's message that they decode (5 points). If they decode their message or another team's message entirely, they get a bonus (10 points).

A-3. If time permits, you might suggest running this encoding/decoding game again, using skills developed the first time. You could also provide the following suggestions:

Teams could make code wheels to assign one letter of the alphabet to another.

They could group all the encoded letters in groups of three so other teams couldn't figure out which are the two-letter or one-letter words.

They could agree to throw in a random letter every fifth character, or throw it in at some changing position (second position, fourth position, sixth position, . . .).

DEPARTURE

Challenge them to devise more elaborate codes at home and to try them with longer messages. They can work with their friends to try to decode each other's messages.

REFERENCES

C. Samuel Micklus, *Problems! Problems! Problems!* Glassboro, NJ: Creative Competitions, 1990.

HATS

OVERVIEW
Teams of two or three kids design and make mock-up hats.

TOOLS AND MATERIALS
Denim cloth ($\frac{1}{2}$ yard per team), cardboard cereal boxes (1 per team), duct tape (1 roll), scissors (1 pair per team), rulers. All the hats you can borrow (have each Guide bring in their wackiest hats from home).

OPENING
Have kids form in pairs to draw a story about a "Hero Hat." Each member of a pair has three minutes to sketch and tell a story simultaneously about a hat that saved the day. They should include in their sketch all the action that occurs and, of course, the hat and any special features it has. When they have finished, the other team member gets his/her turn.

REVIEW
Check to see if anyone has progressed further with any previous projects.

DEMONSTRATION
Look at each sample hat, how it was made, what its function is, and how it could be improved. Ask the kids how they would convert each into an up-to-date fashion statement.

READING
Hats: "I've Got You Covered," page 95

ACTIVITY

Teams of two or three kids design and then make a hat. Before they can start making their hat, they have to show a design drawing and a name for their hat to a Guide. Their objective should be to make the most creative or most functional (for some specific use) hat possible.

At the end of the lesson, each team is to model their hat and point out its special features. They should address the marketing questions: Who will buy it? How much will they pay for it? Where will it sell?

DEPARTURE

Challenge them to keep working on their hats (they can take their mock-ups with them) and bring them in next session. Point out that hats are big business as promotional items as well as fashion statements and protection from the environment, so they could devise a new hat to promote a pizza restaurant or other store.

REFERENCES

C. Samuel Micklus, *Problems! Problems! Problems!* Glassboro, NJ: Creative Competitions, 1990.

I'M FALLING

OVERVIEW
Teams of kids make parachutes and test them.

TOOLS AND MATERIALS
Plastic sheets or bags of various sizes, lightweight cloth, masking tape, string, scissors (1 per team), large screw nuts (for weights, 1 per team) and a stopwatch. Demonstration: 1" and 3" Styrofoam balls (1 of each), napkin (1), book (1), coffee filters (5), index cards (2), pennies (2), hot glue gun, measuring tape.

OPENING
Have washers out on the table and ask early arrivals to test if a washer flicked will hit the ground at the same time as one dropped (from the same height). Have one kid flick a washer near the edge of a table at the same time another lightly pushes an identical washer off the edge. A third kid can judge if they get to the floor at the same time. Can they devise a simple mechanism to drop and launch the two washers at exactly the same instant? (They have to make sure that the launching doesn't give the washer an upward acceleration.)

REVIEW
See if anyone has brought in an advanced project from home.

DEMONSTRATION
This series of demonstrations will show how air resistance manifests itself on falling objects.

D-1. Hold up a paper napkin and a heavy book. Ask which will fall to the floor faster. "Aren't both objects being pulled at the same rate of acceleration?" If the consensus is that they will fall at the same speed, drop both side by side. If the consensus is that the book will fall faster, place the napkin on top of the book and drop the book. When air resistance is important, the size and weight of objects influence how fast they fall. (In a vacuum, both the napkin and book would fall at the same rate.)

D-2. "Does the shape of an object make a difference in its falling speed?" Drop two pieces of paper, one crumpled and one flat. Mass alone doesn't determine the rate of fall when air resists the fall.

D-3. "Does the orientation into the wind make a difference?" Drop two index cards, each having a penny glued to them. One has the penny glued in the middle and the other has it glued at one edge. "What happens if you hold your hand out a car window. (This can be dangerous.) At what orientation do you most feel the most wind resistance?" Orientation matters.

D-4. Hold up two Styrofoam balls: a 1"- and a 3"-diameter ball. Ask which will hit the ground first. For the first trial, hold them about 3' off the ground. Then try at greater heights. Air resistance depends on the surface area. Although the larger ball has a greater surface area, its weight increased at a faster rate than its area did (area increases as the square of the radius, while the volume and weight increases with the cube of the radius). A tiny fleck of Styrofoam floats to the ground and a giant ball comes crashing down. As the ball size gets bigger, its acceleration approaches "g." For small balls, wind resistance is more important and acceleration is smaller than "g."

D-5. Wind resistance increases with the square of the wind speed. That is, if you double the wind speed, you increase the resistance fourfold. Drop a coffee filter from three feet above the ground and four nested coffee filters from six feet about the ground. They will land at the same time. So the nested filters have twice the velocity (they travel twice as far in the same length of time).

"If this stack of filters had twice the velocity, how many filters are in the stack?" Since the air resistance is proportional to the velocity squared and since the resistance is balanced by the force of gravity, the mass of the filters has to be four times as much as the single filter (since it fell twice as fast—2 squared is 4). (It may help to draw a picture showing the height of the two releases and the balance of forces for each.) Count out the four filters from the stack.

This assumes that the two stacks have accelerated to their terminal velocity—that is, that they are no longer accelerating—and that the wind resistance is balanced by the gravitational attraction. If you repeated this experiment from a drop height of only a few inches, they would still be accelerating when they landed and wouldn't land at the same time.

READING

Oh, Chute! (Parachutes), page 101

ACTIVITY

The challenge is to build and test parachutes that land the payload (the nut) at the slowest speed possible. Check out safe launch areas prior to the activity and prepare the Guides to conduct the launching for you. Have them also measure the height of the launch site so each team can compute the average velocity of its parachute drop.

Teams of two or three kids can work together to pick materials and design and build parachutes. Give them time to test several models before the final test. Make sure the Guides open the chutes before dropping them during the test.

One Guide drops the chutes while another measures the time of fall (using a stopwatch). If time permits, do two drops for each team and have them average the times. Have teams also compute the average velocity (since the initial velocity is zero: they divide distance of the fall by time elapsed, and they get an average velocity).

The parachute with the lowest velocity is the best parachute by this criteria.

DEPARTURE

Challenge them to continue trying designs for parachutes at home and to bring in any especially good ones—any with average speeds lower than the slower speeds achieved during the lesson.

REFERENCES

Robert Ehrlich, *Turning the World Inside Out.* Princeton, NJ: Princeton University Press, 1990. This book has great demonstrations, including several on air resistance.

George Pfiffner, *Earth-friendly Toys.* New York: John Wiley & Sons, 1994. This book shows how to make a parachute from a bandana.

Beverley Taylor, James Poth, and Dwight Portman, *Teaching Physics with Toys.* New York: TAB Books/McGraw-Hill, 1995. The coffee filter demonstration is presented as a laboratory experience.

TIME IS ON OUR SIDE

OVERVIEW

Time plays a central role in our lives—we regulate our lives by clocks and watches. Yet, few people understand how we measure time. In this activity, participants create their own time-keeping devices and determine how accurate they are.

TOOLS AND MATERIALS

Two-liter soft drink bottles (10), milk containers (5), small funnels (3), sand (5 pounds), newspaper (to put under projects so cleanup is easier), duct tape, stopwatch, bucket, water, nails of various sizes, small diameter plastic hose to siphon water, time-keeping devices to demonstrate.

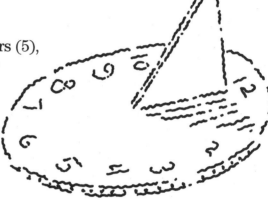

OPENING

Challenge kids to list as many devices at home, on the street, in businesses, and at school that use time-keeping devices as they can. See which team of kids can come up with the most comprehensive list. Here are a few for your reference:

> *at home:* VCRs, cooking timers, oven, lawn sprinklers
> *on the street:* traffic lights, parking meters
> *in businesses:* punch clocks, bank vault locks
> *in schools:* class period bells

REVIEW

Check to see who continued work on the most recent project at home.

DEMONSTRATION

Show as many different types of timing devices as possible. Start with a simple string and weight pendulum. Ask them how to adjust the length to get it to swing exactly once per second. Once you have it swinging once per second, ask how they could use it to measure a minute (by counting 60 seconds).

Build a sundial out of cardboard. The important points are that you orient it due north (due south in the Southern Hemisphere) and, ideally, that the gnomon (the part that casts a shadow) has its upper surface at an angle with the base that is the same as your latitude. In Fresno, California, the latitude is about 37° N, so the gnomon should make a 37° angle with the base. If you can supply materials for kids to take home, they can make sundials there and calibrate them by making marks every hour. (The inquisitive student may want to use the sundial throughout the year to see how the length of the shadow changes and how the duration of hours changes.)

Show the principles of a water clock by using a siphon to draw water out of a bucket into a 2-liter bottle. When the water level reaches some mark on the bottle, record the time. Empty the bottle and repeat it to see how consistent it is.

Demonstrate egg timers or hourglasses to show that materials other than water (sand) can work in timers. Also show watches and any other devices you can find.

READING
Use one of the previously unread stories.

ACTIVITY
Teams of three or four design and build devices that will measure one minute as accurately as possible. They can use pendulums, water clocks, sand clocks, or other devices of their own construction.

After 20 minutes, have a "time off" to see how accurately each team's device is. You start the stopwatch and yell "go!" Team members raise their hands when their device indicates that one minute has elapsed. Inventing guides record how accurate each team was. You might want to repeat the test.

Talk about which design worked best and ask the kids why they think one did better than another. Then challenge them to build a five-minute timer based on the same principles as their one-minute timer.

They could stack 5 one-minute timers on top of one another, or they could make one device that is much larger. Hold a "time off" for five-minute clocks and discuss the results. Ask them how they would scale up to measure an hour or a day. Would their approach work?

DEPARTURE
Challenge the kids to think of other ways to keep time and to bring in their projects for the next session.

REFERENCES
Kay Davies and Wendy Oldfield, *The Super Science Book of Time*. Stamford, CT: Thomson Learning, 1992.
Bernie Zubrowski, *Clocks*. New York: Beech Tree, 1988.

AUTOROTATE

OVERVIEW

We are obsessed with things that move fast, but in this activity we focus on moving slowly. Specifically, we focus on things that fall slowly. What makes something fall slower than something else? Who can design and build the slowest falling device?

TOOLS AND MATERIALS

Scissors, pencils, scrap office paper, index cards, a Ping-Pong™ ball and a rubber ball about the same size, 2 identical balls (tennis balls), 2 pennies, plastic loop (2), tape, card stock or cardboard from cereal boxes.

OPENING

Challenge kids to make paper airplanes that stay aloft the longest time. Hold a fly-off as the session begins.

REVIEW

Check to see who continued work on the most recent project at home.

DEMONSTRATION

(Repeat some of the demonstrations conducted for "I'm Falling.") Start by asking kids which of two identical pieces of paper will fall fastest to the ground. They probably will say that they will fall at the same rate. Then, as you are about to drop them, crumple one in your hand and then drop both. Tell them: "I was right. This one fell faster." Let them tell you how you cheated. Obviously, the shape of an object impacts the rate of fall.

You could repeat this with two plastic bags, one with the added weight of two paper clips (on the handles or the lip) and the other without. "Which will fall faster, the heavier or lighter bag?" It depends on how you release them: open up the bag with paper clips so it falls like a parachute and crumple the other one into as small a ball as you can.

In addition to shape, what else matters when thinking about things that fall? How about orientation? Take two index cards and tape a penny to each: place the penny in the center of one and at one of the narrower edges of the other. Have students predict which will fall faster. Then drop both.

Take the Ping-Pong ball and rubber ball and ask kids which will fall faster. Then drop both from a height of about 3'. Did they fall together? Keep raising the height of release until the rubber ball arrives noticeably sooner. Why do they fall at the same rate for short distances, but different rates for longer distances? (You may need a ladder or stairs to reach heights—say 12'—that give noticeable differences.) Air resistance is increasingly important as the air speed (or relative speed, since the balls are moving through the air) increases. As speed increases, resistance increases at the rate of the speed squared. The impact of air resistance is much greater for less dense objects, like the Ping-Pong ball or a bubble or balloon, and they fall slower.

Which will hit the floor first, a ball that drops from the table or one that rolls off the table? Make a trough out of cardboard so you can have one ball accelerate by gravity. Aim the trough at the second ball located at the edge of the table. When you release the first ball, it will roll down and impact the second one shooting it across the room, while the first one falls to the floor. Which will hit first?

READING
Spin to Fly (Igor Sikorsky), page 108

ACTIVITY
Teams of three or four design and build devices out of paper to fall the slowest. One possible way is to make autogyros. Two patterns are attached. If kids elect to make autogyros, they can try different designs and sizes to see which works best. Hold a "drop off" at the end of the session to see which design falls slowest. You might try dropping them from different heights to see if they perform differently at different heights.

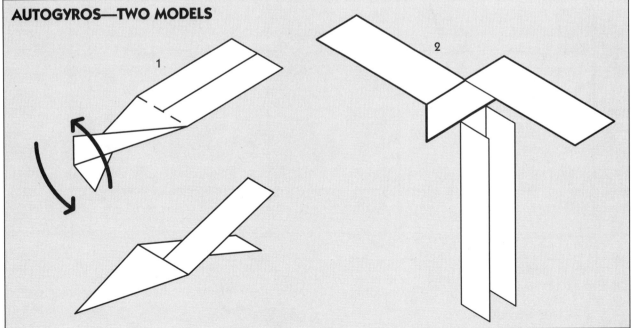

AUTOGYROS—TWO MODELS

AUTO ROTATOR

Copyright © 1999 Addison-Wesley Educational Publishers, Inc.

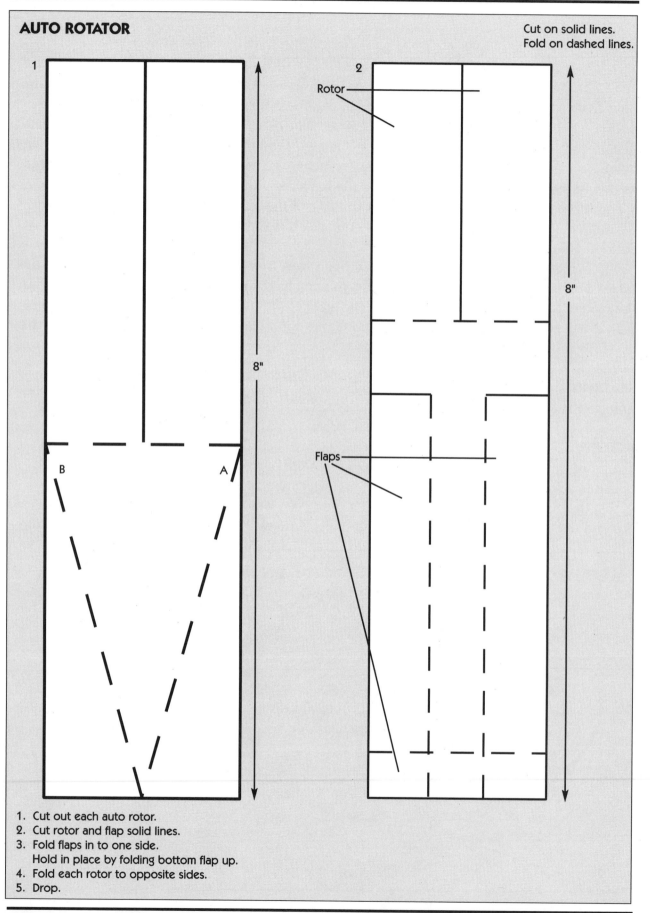

Cut on solid lines.
Fold on dashed lines.

8"

8"

Rotor

Flaps

A

B

1. Cut out each auto rotor.
2. Cut rotor and flap solid lines.
3. Fold flaps in to one side.
   Hold in place by folding bottom flap up.
4. Fold each rotor to opposite sides.
5. Drop.

DEPARTURE

Challenge students to make autogyros with four or more arms from paper.

REFERENCES

Robert Ehrlich, *Turning the World Inside Out*. Princeton, NJ: Princeton University Press, 1990.

The Sky's the Limit with Math and Science. Fresno, CA: AIMS Activities in Aerodynamics, 1987.

SECTION 2
STORIES FOR YOUNG INVENTORS

A WONDERFUL MISTAKE

When you think of an invention, you may imagine someone working in a laboratory conducting experiments while they search for the solution to a problem. However, as strange as it may seem, many inventions result from the mistakes people make.

One such invention is something with which you are familiar. In fact, you probably love to eat them. Lots of them. In the United States we eat seven billion of them a year.

What do you think this invention is? What food product do you think we eat seven billion of in one year?

This great invention is the chocolate chip cookie, or by its proper name, the Toll House Cookie®. And, like so many other inventions, it was discovered when someone made a mistake.

The someone was Ruth Wakefield. The mistake occurred one day when Mrs. Wakefield was making her favorite chocolate butter drop cookies. She was making them at the Toll House Inn in Massachusetts that she and her husband owned.

Who can find Massachusetts on the map? In what part of the country is it located?

On this day in 1933, Mrs. Wakefield was in a hurry, and rather than melting the chunks of chocolate before adding them to the cookie dough, she just mixed the unmelted chunks into her dough and put the cookies in the oven to bake. She expected that the chocolate would melt during baking and would mix with the dough to make the same chocolate butter drop cookies, but with less work on her part. She was wrong.

What do most people do when they make mistakes? (They go back and start over.) People who are inventive ask questions. They want to know why a mistake occurred and if they can learn something from it.

Although she was an innkeeper, Mrs. Wakefield was also an inventor. She sampled her mistakes and found them to be delicious. She named her invention after the inn, Toll House Cookies.

It took several years for the Nestlé Company to recognize that they could sell more chocolate if they made their semi-sweet chocolate in tiny chunks that bakers could use to make Toll House Cookies. Eventually they started making the chocolate chips and were so successful that they bought the name, Toll House Cookie, from Mrs. Wakefield. Today you can still find Mrs. Wakefield's recipe on the back of packages of Nestlé's Semi-Sweet Morsels.

BEFORE THE BULB

When you think of Thomas Edison, you probably think of an old man with white hair, already famous for his many inventions. But before Edison was a famous inventor, he had been an inquisitive child.

Edison was born in Milan (pronounced *my-lin*), Ohio, in 1847. As a young boy he liked to ask questions: "Why does water put out fire?" and "What makes birds fly?" When he found that people didn't know the answers to a question he would devise an experiment to find the answer. Sometimes he got into trouble with his experiments.

Let's find Milan, Ohio, on the map. Who knows where Ohio is? (Milan is just south of Lake Erie, about midway across the state). What are the surrounding states?

When he was seven years old, his family moved to Port Huron, Michigan, and Thomas entered public school for the first time. He wasn't in school for long. He asked so many questions that he got into trouble. His teacher thought Thomas wasn't smart enough for school, so Mrs. Edison withdrew him from school and started teaching him at home.

Do you know someone who stays at home to learn? Do you think you would learn well at home?

Mrs. Edison had the idea that learning should be fun. Instead of teaching him, she encouraged him to explore as a path to learning. By nine years of age, Edison had a well-stocked chemistry laboratory in his home and was conducting lots of experiments.

He learned to send messages on a telegraph and got a job as a telegraph operator. His first invention was a device to send a message automatically on the telegraph. His next invention was an electric device to count votes at elections. When he couldn't sell the vote tabulator, he promised himself not to waste his time inventing something he couldn't sell.

Edison went on to an illustrious career. He was awarded 1,093 patents for devices such as the phonograph (record player), electric light bulb, motion picture camera and projector, and many others. Not everything in his life turned out wonderfully, and Edison had his share of failures. But the inquisitive boy from Milan, Ohio, changed the world with his inventive ideas.

Would it be fun to be an inventor? Today you need to have good training in science and engineering as well as an inquisitive mind.

BLAST OFF

Can you imagine a man so far advanced beyond others in his field that people didn't recognize his genius? Such a man was the inventor of modern rocketry, Robert Goddard.

Goddard was not the first person to launch rockets. Historians believe that the Chinese army used rockets as weapons as early as A.D. 1232. These rockets burned a black powder similar to gunpowder. The British army used rockets against the Americans in the War of 1812, and the sight of their "red glare" inspired Francis Scott Key to write the "Star Spangled Banner." Both the North and South used them in the Civil War, but these rockets weren't all that effective. Furthermore, these rockets were too crude for scientific research or space exploration.

Goddard obtained his Ph.D. in 1911 and started his lifelong research on rockets. When he wrote an article describing what would be needed to send a rocket ship to the moon, many people thought he was crazy. They thought it would be impossible for people to get to the moon. Goddard received so much negative reaction to his ideas that he avoided public exposure of his research for the rest of his career.

If you had an idea that you thought was really good but no one else liked it, what would you do? Would you give up? Would you decide that maybe your idea wasn't any good?

The experience with the article led Goddard to avoid publicity, but he kept working on his research. Along the way he had many failures. He was trying to get rockets to fly higher and be more reliable than ever before, and there was no one he could turn to for help. So he had to try each idea to see if it worked.

In 1926 Goddard designed the first liquid propellant rocket and that led him to try building larger rockets. To stabilize his rockets and keep them flying on course, he had to invent a gyroscope system. During World War II, he helped design a jet-assisted takeoff device for Navy planes. Over the course of his research, Goddard earned 214 patents.

Although people didn't appreciate his contributions to science while Goddard was alive, today we recognize him as the father of modern rocketry and space flight.

Do people always appreciate new inventions? Can you think of any other inventions that people didn't think were worthwhile? One is the copy machine. When it was invented no one wanted to make it. Today, copy machines are an essential part of life in most businesses and schools. Often new ideas and new things aren't accepted right away. It can take time before people see the value in them.

BOUNCING BACK FROM ADVERSITY

One of the great inventions of modern times was made by accident. The inventor of this discovery never profited from his invention, but we remember his name today: Charles Goodyear.

Charles Goodyear labored for more than a decade to transform raw rubber into a useful product. Rubber is derived from a milky substance in plants. When you break the stem of a dandelion, you see this substance, called latex, ooze out. Latex is composed of water and rubber. Indians in Central and South America learned how to use latex to waterproof bottles. Europeans found out how to use it to waterproof clothing. The problem with this rubber was that it melted in summer, cracked in the cold of winter, and stuck to whatever it came in contact with. So scientists set out to find ways to improve natural rubber. And no scientist was more persistent than Charles Goodyear.

After about six years of experiments, Goodyear developed a method that improved rubber somewhat. During this work he didn't have a job, so his family was poor. One time he was thrown in prison because he hadn't paid his debts. He always overcame adversity and continued his research on rubber.

Later he discovered the process of vulcanization when he spilled a mixture of rubber and sulfur on a hot stove. In cleaning up the mess, he discovered that it had the properties he sought and he got a patent in 1844.

How many times we do make mistakes and never allow ourselves to ask if there is something valuable in the mistake? Many inventions and discoveries are made when people look at accidents and mistakes and find something worthwhile.

Unfortunately for Goodyear, other people used his method of vulcanization and didn't pay him a royalty as they should have. Although he made a great contribution to science, he died a poor man.

Today there are many products made from natural and synthetic rubber—that is, rubber that is made from chemicals rather than from the latex in rubber trees.

What can you think of that is made of rubber? (The elastic in your socks and under-wear, rubber bands, rubber gaskets around car windows, backing on floor mats. . . .)

Bungee cords are made from rubber. First they were used just to hold things down. But in 1979, an Englishman started a new sport using bungee cords.

Do you know what the sport is? Has anyone that you know ever tried bungee jumping? It can be very dangerous, so don't try it unless you are with a professional jumper who has lots of experience.

In bungee jumping a person attaches a very strong bungee cord, like a giant rubber band, to straps on his or her ankles and chest. Bungee jumpers jump off a bridge or other high places and after free-falling, the bungee cord slows them down and bounces them back up. All the energy of position, when the person is standing on the bridge, is ultimately converted into heat inside the bungee cord, which stretches 3 or 4 times its unstretched length. Quite a rush.

Does bungee jumping sound like fun to anyone? That would be pretty scary, wouldn't it? Well, we're going to try some bungee jumping in a few minutes, only we'll use an egg instead of one of us.

The world record distance for bungee jumping off a fixed structure is 822'.

BUILDING A MONOPOLY ON BOARD GAMES

Who likes playing board games? Which are your favorite ones? Can you guess what the all-time best-selling modern board game is? The best-selling twentieth-century game is Monopoly®. (Chess, Parcheesi, and Checkers were developed hundreds of years ago.)

Monopoly was an invention built out of the depths of the economic depression. An unemployed engineer, Charles Darrow, started designing a game to pass his time. He had no intention of selling the game; he just wanted to make a game that was fun to play.

Could you invent a game? How long would it take to get it perfect?

It took Darrow several years to come up with the design of Monopoly—he would try a new idea and play the game with friends for a while and then try another idea. By 1933 Darrow had put the game together.

Monopoly reflects the economic conditions of the times and the geography where Darrow lived. He patterned the board after Atlantic City, New Jersey, where Darrow had vacationed. He got the names for the streets from street names in Atlantic City. Because money was tight during the Depression, Darrow made it easy to get money in the game. And since he read daily in the newspaper about businesses failing and banks taking over properties, he focused the game on accumulating and losing titles to property. As in most board games, there is an element of luck, and Darrow added dice and chance cards to include it.

Who knows were Atlantic City is? Let's find it on a map.

If you were going to invent a game, what would you put in it? Would you use the streets of your town? Would you include other things from your life, like school, home, stores and malls, cars? What else would you include?

Darrow played the game with friends and his family. They liked it so much they convinced him to try to sell it to a game manufacturer. When he did, he was turned down.

What would you do if your invention was turned down by the experts? Would you give up? Can you think of something else that Darrow could have done?

Although discouraged, Darrow decided to try to make and sell the game himself. He made 5,000 sets and sold them quickly—so quickly that a game manufacturer heard about it and bought the rights. Parker Brothers, a company that had originally rejected the game, bought it and paid Charles Darrow royalties.

Do you know what royalties are? (They are payments given to an artist, musician, or inventor for their creative products.) Our constitution gives us the right to profit from our creative products.

Charles Darrow became a very rich man. Parker Brothers sold millions of sets of Monopoly and made millions of dollars also. The game is sold throughout the world and has outsold every other game made during this century. Not bad for an idea that came to Charles Darrow while he was just passing the time of day.

BUTTON UP

*Teachers Note: If possible, have some Velcro®
ready to demonstrate.*

One of the first inventions humans made was
clothing. Even today, after hundreds of
thousands of years of thinking about and
improving clothes, new ideas come along to make
them better.

Think about just one aspect of clothes:
fasteners.

*How many different ways can you
think of to fasten clothes? (Buttons, belts,
zippers, Velcro, shoelaces, snaps. . . .) Each of
these was invented by one or several people and improved or changed by many others.*

One of the most recently invented fasteners is Velcro.

Do you know how Velcro works?

One side has tiny hooks and the other side has tiny loops. No one hook and loop
would be strong enough to hold a coat shut. But, by having many of them, they are strong
enough. And, in many cases the Velcro system is much easier to use than tying a lace, and
much more effective against wind than buttons would be.

*Do you have clothing that has Velcro fasteners? What kind of clothing is it? (Shoes,
coats, hats, . . .)*

How do you imagine someone came up with the idea for Velcro?

A man from Switzerland, George de Mestral, noticed that his dog was often covered
with burs from weeds in the Alps. The burs were like hooks that attached to the curly fur of
his dog. He didn't think about it right away, but later, when he had trouble closing a zipper,
he thought there must be a better way to close clothing, and he remembered the burs.

It took Mr. de Mestral six years to develop Velcro and a way to manufacture it. One
of the things he had to discover was how many loops were needed. He found that he needed to make 300 loops per square inch to make it hold well.

*Here is the area of about one square inch. Imagine 300 loops in this area. Next
time you use your Velcro clothing, look at the pieces closely to see how many loops and
hooks there are in a square inch.*

He came up with the name Velcro as a combination of two words: *vel* from *velvet* and *cro* from the French word for "small hook."

Mr. de Mestral started inventing when he was 12 years old. His first patent was for a toy airplane. He had many other inventions during his life.

Are you too young to invent?

Can you think of a new piece of clothing or a new fastener for clothes? Do you think you could come up with an idea right away, or would it take you a long time to come up with one? Did Mr. de Mestral realize how to use the idea of the bur and dog hair right away? (It took him several months. It wasn't until he faced a problem, a balky zipper, that he thought of the solution. In this case the solution came before he recognized the problem.)

COLLISIONS

Percy Julian collided with the system of his times. People often fail when they collide with a system of long-held views, but Julian succeeded.

Julian was the grandson of a slave. He was an African American when African Americans weren't given the same rights as other people in this country. Julian wasn't allowed to go to school after the eighth grade.

What would you do if you couldn't go to school after the eighth grade? Could you get a job without an education? What work could you do without an education? Luckily for you, you can attend school.

Although Julian hadn't graduated from high school, DePauw University allowed him to enter college. He proved their decision a wise one when he graduated in 1920 as class valedictorian, the student with the highest grades. He taught college chemistry and got his Master's degree from Harvard.

Julian collided with the system when he wanted to get his doctorate degree in organic chemistry. He had to go to Europe to get his degree as colleges in this country wouldn't accept him because he was black. When he came back to the United States, DePauw University wouldn't hire him because he was black.

What do you think about someone being denied an opportunity because of his or her race? Is that fair?

Julian went on to make great scientific accomplishments. He found a way to make a drug to treat glaucoma, a disease of the eyes. He developed a way to coat and treat paper and to make cold-water paints, and he found a new product to put out fires. He found ways to make (synthesize) useful drugs, most importantly Cortisone. This invention reduced the price of this drug from hundreds of dollars per drop to pennies per drop.

After he was so successful, do you think he would be angry at DePauw University for not letting him teach there?

Recognizing his great accomplishments and the changing attitudes in the country, DePauw University invited Julian to sit on their governing board. He accepted.

Percy Julian was a great American inventor and scientist.

ELEVATORS—HOW TO GET UP IN THE WORLD

Imagine standing in the crowd of people at the New York Fair in 1854 watching a demonstration. A man was standing in an elevator while it was being raised. The elevator had been built with an open-sided shaft so people could look in to see the man inside.

The idea for elevators in buildings had been around for a long time. Archimedes invented one in 230 B.C. using ropes. It was able to lift one person. For many centuries there was little interest in elevators since buildings were generally only one story or floor. But as cities got more crowded in the late 1800s, people started making buildings taller. The question of "How tall could you make a building?" really became a question of "For how many floors will someone be willing to walk up the stairs?"

Who has ridden an elevator? How tall was the building? Can you imagine having to visit someone at the top of a ten-story building and not having an elevator?

Although elevators were usually safe, occasionally one would fall. The cables would break and down it would come, injuring or killing anyone inside.

Has anyone thought about falling while riding an elevator? Does riding make you nervous? If so, you can be thankful for the inventor we are going to read about.

Since people were anxious about riding elevators and since they didn't want to climb many flights of stairs, buildings weren't being built very tall. This meant that cities had to grow outward, taking up more valuable land. All that changed at the New York World's Fair.

Standing in the elevator at the fair was Elisha G. Otis. He was an engineer and inventor. Later in life he invented a steam plow and an oven for baking. After his assistants had raised him up in the elevator, Otis cut the cables holding the elevator. The crowd gasped.

What do you think happened next? If he fell and killed himself would we be reading this story? Have you ever heard of the Otis Elevator Company? Do you think he was saved?

The elevator hardly dropped at all. Otis had invented an automatic brake for elevators. When he cut the cables, the elevator started to fall but then the brakes held. Otis hadn't invented the elevator, but he invented the device that made elevators safe.

With Otis's invention of the automatic elevator brake, architects started designing taller buildings and having elevators installed. So when you ride in an elevator, think about Elisha Otis and his invention of the safety brake.

FROM CASTLES TO KEVLAR®

Castles were invented to protect people and their belongings. At first they were mounds of dirt. Later, castle builders used wood posts, and still later they used stone.

As castles became more difficult for a band of thieves or an army to penetrate, the thieves and armies developed better technology too. Catapults were one way to break down the defenses of a castle.

At first soldiers might bend a tree over and use it as a springy launcher. Later designs got more complex and were capable of launching larger loads.

As catapults got better, what do you think castle builders did? (They built the walls taller and stronger.)

Both the attackers and defenders continually had to improve designs to keep up with their opponents. Eventually, the launchers won. With bigger catapults and gun powder and cannons, castles, however strong they were, became too easy a target for attacking armies. So people stopped building castles.

The same type of arms race continues today. One army builds a better offensive weapon and the other builds a better way to defend against it.

One invention used to protect people from injuries today is Kevlar®. Kevlar is a polymer (a man-made fiber with really long molecule chains) used to make ropes, boats, and bullet-resistant vests. Pound for pound, it is five times stronger than steel.

Stephanie Kwolek invented kevlar. She started working for Du Pont in 1946 as a chemist. At that time there were few women who worked in laboratories and she wanted to prove she could do chemistry well. She did—her name is on 17 patents. Kwolek is a pioneer in polymer chemistry.

Chemists, like Stephanie Kwolek, are trying to discover new fibers and chemicals to protect people and to make life safer. You might think that after many years of research there would be nothing more to discover, but just as Kwolek found a new type of fiber that no one had thought of before, there are many new discoveries waiting for you to find them.

Do you think if castle builders had Kevlar that they would still be building castles?

HATS: "I'VE GOT YOU COVERED"

Hats protect us from the dangers of our environment and also make fashion statements about us. Undoubtedly the first hats were fashioned from natural materials to shield the wearer from a sudden burst of rain or provide warmth on a frosty morning. Today, hats are as varied as the people on this planet.

Think of all the different styles of hats you have seen. Who can name one? (Cowboy ten-gallon hats, a king's crown, baseball caps, helmets, fashion hats. . . .)

In hot, sunny climates hats evolved to have wide brims, like sombreros. To serve the same function in this country, John Stetson invented the ten-gallon cowboy hat. In cold climates wool or animal fur is preferred, and some of these hats have built-in earflaps. Construction workers, firefighters, and football players wear hard hats to protect their heads from injuries. Baseball players wear hard hats only when they are batting and wear caps when they are on the field to shield their eyes from the sun.

Can you think of hats that symbolize a position of authority or are worn as part of a religion?

A matador wears a unique hat, just as an Amish person does. Park rangers have distinctive hats that you can recognize in a second. A king or queen wears a crown as a symbol of their position, and court jesters wore hats to make people laugh. Bishops and other religious leaders have hats signifying their rank.

How many different kinds of hats do you imagine there are?

Fedora, Panama, Derby and Stetson®, bonnet, skullcap, stovepipe, tam-o'shanter, top hat, turban, fez, dunce cap, bowler, and beret are just some of the types of hats. One reference listed more than 80 different kinds. And these don't include special hats worn for sports like football, hockey, hiking, and more. Each style of hat was developed by an inventor or designer to meet some special need.

We know that people in cold climates were wearing hoods as much as 100,000 years ago. Five thousand years ago, Egyptian nobles were wearing crowns. The first hats with brims were made by Greek people around 500 B.C. As societies developed, hats were designed to make fashion statements and, at least for some people, ceased to serve a useful function. In the 1700s in Europe, women started wearing hats for decoration and added ribbons, feathers, lace, and flowers.

There are so many kinds and styles of hats that you might think that there is no room for improvement or refinement. But there is. Start a new style or incorporate a new material in a hat and you could have a great invention. So think about a need not met or a fashion style not yet visualized and you could be the next mad hatter.

HOT STUFF

So many inventions have resulted from mistakes that you might think you need to make mistakes to be a successful inventor. Indeed, Thomas Edison said that making mistakes was a fundamental part of success in that each mistake becomes a stepping stone to the eventual solution of a problem.

A great example of a mistake turning into an invention is the microwave oven.

Does everyone know what a microwave oven is? (It is an oven that heats food by sending energy in the form of radio waves. Because of their small size, the radio waves are called microwaves. They vibrate the water inside food and these vibrations heat the food.) Who has one at home? What do you like about using it?

The microwave oven was invented when an engineer made a mistake. Percy Spencer was carrying a candy bar in his pants pocket while working in his lab. He was conducting experiments on a new type of vacuum tube, a device that emits radiation.

When Percy got hungry, he stuck his hand into his pocket and found a gooey mess. The candy bar had melted and he had no idea of why it had melted.

What would you have done if you found that your candy bar had melted? Would you have cleaned up the mess and gone on with your work? Or, would you have asked some questions about why the candy bar melted?

Percy tried to figure out why the candy bar had melted. The room wasn't hot and he hadn't been standing near anything that was hot. He figured that it must have been caused by the new vacuum tube he was testing. So he decided to run an experiment.

He placed some corn kernels in front of the tube and turned it on. In a few seconds the kernels were popping. Then he tried a raw egg. When he turned on the tube, the egg exploded. He figured out that the tube had heated the inside of the egg and before the expanding gas inside could escape, the pressure from the gas exploded the egg.

The company Percy worked for, Raytheon, started to build the new "Radarrange." Like many new products it sold slowly at first. Today, however, there are millions of microwave ovens in operation all over the world.

For the invention of the microwave oven, we can thank Mr. Percy Spencer, his melted candy bar, and most important, his curiosity.

Asking questions is one of the most important parts of being an inventor or scientist. You might practice asking questions and see what you can learn. Ask them especially when a mistake occurs.

HOW TELECOMMUNICATIONS GOT STARTED

Samuel Morse wanted to be a painter, not a scientist. He had little training in science and spent much of his professional career as a struggling painter. But when he was not able to support himself by painting, he turned to inventing.

Morse invented pumps for fire engines and a tool for cutting marble for statues. It is for his invention of the telegraph, however, that we remember him.

Who knows what a telegraph is? (It is an electric system for sending messages long distances. Operators turn on and off switches very quickly to form dots and dashes—either as sounds or marks on paper. These dots and dashes represent letters and numbers that a trained operator can translate into words and messages.)

Although Morse had learned the basics about the "new science" of electricity in the early 1800s, he knew very little about it. His lack of knowledge made it harder for him to develop the telegraph.

In 1835 Morse began to work on the telegraph system, and two years later he had one capable of sending messages 10 miles. That same year the U. S. Congress called for proposals to make a new communications system to connect New York and New Orleans, and Morse was the only person to propose an electric system.

It took several more years for Congress to recognize the potential of Morse's system, and in 1844 he demonstrated his system by sending his famous message from Baltimore to Washington, D.C. The message was: "What hath God wrought!"

What did that mean? (Look at the marvelous things that God has provided us. Morse was a deeply religious man.)

Who knows where Baltimore is? (It's close to Washington, D.C., to the east. How about New Orleans? New Orleans was the cotton market, and Congress wanted to be able to communicate information more quickly to the financial center of New York.)

To send messages on the telegraph system, Morse had to devise a code. We call it the Morse code. Each letter and number are assigned an arrangement of short and long pulses. For example, the letter "a" is dot-dash. The letter "s" is dot-dot-dot. He assigned simpler codes for the more commonly used letters to make sending messages faster. Later, when radio was invented, Morse code was used there . . . and is still used for some types of radio broadcasting.

By 1861 the East and West coasts of the United States were linked by telegraph wires. This was the dawn of telecommunications that has evolved today so just about any-one can talk to just about anyone else anywhere in the world at any time.

Dash/dot-dot-dot-dot/dot Dot/dash-dot/dash-dot-dot

The end

MORSE CODE			
a	dot-dash	o	dash-dash-dash
b	dash-dot-dot-dot	p	dot-dash-dash-dot
c	dash-dot-dash-dot	q	dash-dash-dot-dash
d	dash-dot-dot	r	dot-dash-dot
e	dot	s	dot-dot-dot
f	dot-dot-dash-dot	t	dash
g	dash-dash-dot	u	dot-dot-dash
h	dot-dot-dot-dot	v	dot-dot-dot-dash
i	dot-dot	w	dot-dash-dash
j	dot-dash-dash-dash	x	dash-dot-dot-dash
k	dash-dot-dash	y	dash-dot-dash-dash
l	dot-dash-dot-dot	z	dash-dash-dot-dot
m	dash-dash	end of message	dot-dash-dot-dash-dot
n	dash-dot		

There are additional codes for numbers and punctuation and to indicate an error.

NEW MONEY

Imagine you are a businessperson entertaining a customer in a nice restaurant. At the end of the meal you reach for your money to pay for the dinner, and, to your horror, you discover you left it in your hotel room.

Would you be embarrassed? What would you do?

In this situation in 1950, Frank McNamara did two things. First, he promised to pay the restaurant owner the following day (and he did pay). Second, he invented a system so future diners wouldn't need to carry cash with them.

Can you think of the system McNamara invented?

Working with a friend, McNamara introduced the first multipurpose charge card in early 1950. Some gas station companies had offered credit cards before, but they were only used at that company's station. Mr. McNamara's card, called Diners Club, could be used at lots of different stores and restaurants.

Today, everyone understands how credit cards work. But in 1950, no one did. Do you think people were willing to buy them? Or how about restaurants—do you think they were willing to honor them?

In the first year of operation, McNamara issued cards to 200 people. He got 27 restaurants to honor them. It was a good start. By the end of the following year, more than 42,000 people had paid to have a Diners Club card and 330 businesses accepted them for payment.

Do you think a lot of people carry credit cards? Some people even have several different brands of credit cards.

McNamara started a revolution in credit. Today hundreds of banks issue credit cards and millions of people use them.

The old credit cards are now being replaced by smart cards. These cards carry encoded information that lets the user get money from a bank, make phone calls without coins, and pay for purchases nearly everywhere. They take the place of money.

What started out as an embarrassing situation in a restaurant has grown into a major financial industry and a big convenience for many people. That shows that it pays to take advantage of difficult situations.

OH, CHUTE!

Long before people could fly, they thought of ways to fall safely. Ancient Chinese manuscripts mention parachutes, and Leonardo da Vinci drew pictures of one in 1485. However, it wasn't until 1783 that French physicist Sebastien Lenormand made the first jump. He jumped from a tower. Ten years later another Frenchman, Andre Jacques Garnerin, made the first parachute jump from a flying object, a balloon. He jumped from a height of 2,230 feet and landed safely.

Would you have wanted to make the first jump? Would you have felt comfortable just being in a balloon 2,230 feet above the ground? Balloons were invented only a few months before Lenormand made the first tower jump. Most people living then had never seen them or thought about flying, let alone jumping out of the sky. Would that have been scary?

Parachutes work by providing a large surface for air to drag against. It is the air drag that slows down the parachute jumper. Gravity pulls the jumper toward earth and the drag of air friction slows down the fall. Still, the landing can be rough and it is common for parachutists to sprain ankles or break bones on landing.

Parachutes capable of landing a person must be at least 24 feet in diameter and made of a tough but light material like nylon. Larger parachutes are used to land equipment as large as a truck.

One of the tricks of using a parachute is getting it deployed. Tangled lines could prevent the chute from opening. To ensure that parachutes are packed correctly, they are sent to special companies for packing.

Modern parachutes are shaped to provide lift as well as air resistance. This allows the parachutist to steer toward a landing spot.

Parachute jumping has become a popular sport in this country. Skydivers jump from about 15,000 feet and free-fall as fast as 100 miles per hour. When they get to 2,000 to 3,000 feet above ground, they open their chutes, which slow them to 10 miles per hour.

Is that a sport you would like to try? Okay, let's try it, but we won't use you to test the parachutes.

ONE SMALL INVENTION

When you study about a machine or product to find out who invented it, typically you have a hard time finding the information. Most weren't invented by a single person; the products resulted from a long series of small steps made by different people. For example, Thomas Edison didn't make the first electric light. Several people before him had made them. Edison started with what they had done and made enough improvements so the light burned much longer than anyone else's. Machines like automobiles and computers are the result of thousands of new ideas by many engineers, scientists, and inventors. So it is often difficult to credit a single person with a significant invention.

The two-pronged needle is an exception to this rule. Possibly no other invention has saved so many lives in this century as this needle. The problem that was solved by this needle was how to deliver smallpox vaccine in just the right amount when the shots were given by nonprofessional people. Another part of that problem was there wasn't enough vaccine to meet the needs, especially in poorer countries. Although doctors had created the vaccine to save people, about two million people were still dying of smallpox every year.

Can you imagine two million people dying each year from a disease for which we had the vaccine? Even though we had the vaccine, we weren't able to get it to everyone who needed it. That was a problem that needed an inventor.

Dr. Benjamin Rubin was asked to help solve this problem. After some thought, he tried a simple solution. He ground down the eyelet of a sewing needle to create a two-pronged needle. The needle held just the right amount of vaccine between the two tines, making it easy to vaccinate people.

Do you know what a sewing needle looks like? It has an eye for the thread to pass through. Dr. Rubin removed the top of the needle, so instead of a loop, there were two prongs.

This simple invention helped the World Health Assembly eradicate smallpox. For the first time in history, people had wiped out a disease. Some two million people each year have been saved by this invention.

Most inventions don't have this positive and dramatic an impact. But anyone can work to invent something to make our lives easier, safer or more fulfilling. Ben Rubin did.

PROPEL YOURSELF

Many of the great American inventors were born in other countries. In fact, a high percentage of all the people inducted into the National Inventors Hall of Fame emigrated to the Unites States. Among them are the person who invented the picture tube for television (Zworykin from Russia), the person who invented the artificial heart and kidney (Kolff from the Netherlands), and the person who invented the computer memory (Wang from China).

One of the most prolific foreign-born inventors was John Ericsson. He was born in Sweden in 1803 and came to the United States in 1839. He made over 2,000 inventions (most of which he didn't patent).

Can you imagine inventing 2,000 different things? How would you remember them all? Where would you get all the ideas? You would have to study hard to learn engineering and science and learn language well so you could describe your ideas. And, you would have to work hard, wouldn't you?

We remember Ericsson most of all for two inventions. The first is the propeller for ships. Before his invention of the propeller, ships were propelled either by wind, with sails, or by paddle wheels. Paddle wheels were attached either to the sides of a ship or to the stern. For navy ships this presented a problem as an enemy could knock your ship out of action by hitting the exposed paddle wheel with a cannon shot. Ericsson had a better idea.

His idea was to place the propeller underwater where it was safe from an enemy's gunfire. The propeller was turned by a steam engine inside the ship. Navies and merchant shippers caught on to his idea and started using propellers. Today, almost all ships are propelled this way.

We also remember Ericsson for his invention that changed the course of the Civil War and naval warfare.

Have you heard of the battle of the Monitor *and* Merrimac? *Who can tell the story of these two iron-clad ships? (*Merrimac *was the name of the sunken Union vessel that the Confederates covered with iron plate and rechristened the* CSA Virginia. *There never was a* Monitor-Merrimac *battle; it was the* Monitor-Virginia *battle.)*

John Ericsson designed and supervised the construction of the *Monitor*. He did it in 100 days. The Union had heard about the South's new ship the *Virginia (Merrimac)* and were fearful that it would wreak havoc among their fleet and break the blockade of Southern ports, so they hurried to make their own ironclad ship.

The *Monitor* was the better design. Although the two ships fought to a draw, the design features that Ericsson had incorporated into the *Monitor* worked better and were copied by other naval architects. In 100 days Ericsson changed the way navies designed their warships.

A hundred days sounds like a long time, but new ships and airplanes usually take years and years to design and build. Can you imagine how hard he had to work to finish the job in time?

Ericsson is also remembered for his contributions to the use of compressed air in machines, blowers in boilers, and railroad locomotives.

PUTT-PUTT

You never can predict where great ideas will come from. Take Ole Evinrude. He was rowing a boat two miles across a lake so he could get his girlfriend some ice cream. Of course, since it was a hot day, the ice cream melted by the time he got back to her. That minor misfortune launched Evinrude into action.

How many times have you had a problem and said to yourself that there has to be a better way? Who has a problem they can share with us? How could you solve it? Okay, back to the story.

Evinrude, who had emigrated to America from Norway when he was a young boy, had grown up working with tools. He worked in machine shops building engines and had a love of boats, so he was perfectly suited to invent an outboard motor.

What type of things do you like to do? Who likes sports? Who likes music? You are best qualified to invent things in areas you like. So if you like sports, you may be the right person to invent a new game, or ball, or hockey stick.

Three years after the melted ice cream incident, Evinrude made and tested his first mock-up engine. Later that year he started selling the motors and his wife, the woman who waited for the ice cream, wrote advertisements for them. The business took off and only four years later Evinrude retired.

By thinking about melted ice cream, Evinrude had invented a new machine, the outboard motor, and launched a new industry. Today millions of people around the world enjoy motorboating . . . thanks to Evinrude and his wife.

RECORDING SOUNDS

When you listen to a recording of music you might use a record, a tape, or a CD. Thomas Edison invented the first device to record and play back sounds, the phonograph. The next great advance was recording on magnetic tape, and that advance crushed the career of a budding opera singer.

Other people had recorded sounds magnetically, but the machines were expensive and difficult to use. No one had even thought of recording sounds on magnetic tape; magnetic tape hadn't been invented.

The inventor, Marvin Camras, was an electrical engineering student. Marvin had a cousin, William Korzon, who fancied himself a singer. William thought that if he heard himself sing he could correct his minor flaws and become a great operatic singer. To Marvin this didn't sound like a tough challenge, so he set out to build an inexpensive recorder.

Inventors are always on the lookout for problems to solve. If you want to be an inventor, you need to think of problems you can solve.

While thinking about how to record sounds, Marvin came up with the idea of recording them on a wire. He decided he could magnetize the wire with an electromagnet (a magnet made by passing electricity through coils of wire). He tried it and with some work got it to record and play back sounds.

Do you think Camras would have thought of the solution if he hadn't been thinking about the problem of how to record his cousin's voice? Inventors are always looking for problems to solve.

One technique inventors use to solve problems is to think about them and then go on to other tasks. While they are busy with something else, their mind can continue to work, sometimes coming up with a solution.

The recorder launched Camras's career. He sold recorders to the Navy and kept inventing. Eventually he came up with the magnetic coating used today on recording tapes. Today, Camras has more than 500 patents for his inventions. And it all started by solving one problem for his cousin.

What happened to his cousin? Once he heard his own singing voice, he decided he wasn't cut out to be an opera singer.

SPIN TO FLY

The invention of the airplane is a familiar story, but the invention of the helicopter is less well known.

Who knows how a helicopter flies? What's different between an airplane and a helicopter? Why do you think airplanes are called fixed-wing craft? Do helicopters have fixed wings?

The word *helicopter* was created from Greek words that mean "spiral wings." In helicopters the rotor blades provide lift, just like the wings of an airplane provide lift. Unlike an airplane's wings, the rotors also provide propulsion. Although it looks like it should be easy to build a helicopter, controlling its motion is difficult. Luckily, inventors like Igor Sikorsky had the persistence to follow their dreams.

Like a lot of famous American inventors, Sikorsky wasn't born here. He grew up in Russia and came to the United States after the Russian Revolution. Igor was mechanically inclined and liked to build things, including rubber-band-powered model helicopters. So the things he played with as a boy, helicopters, are things he worked on later as an inventor.

Learning about dirigibles and the Wright Brothers' success inspired Sikorsky to create his own flying machine. In 1913, Sikorsky built the world's first multiengine airplane, a four-engine plane, and flew it above St. Petersburg, Russia. For all his success in Russia, Sikorsky was forced to flee after the communists took over that country in 1917. After a slow start in the United States, Sikorsky gained success in designing a variety of airplanes, including the *American Clipper*, the largest aircraft of its time. One of his airplanes became the first to cross the Pacific Ocean in 1934. Sikorsky eventually turned his attention back to his childhood toy, the helicopter, and made his first successful helicopter flight in 1939.

Igor Sikorsky was a very successful engineer and inventor. The next time you see a helicopter, remember Igor Sikorsky.

Are there things you like to do or play with now that you might like to work on later in life? Would it be fun to design new boats or planes or cars? How about designing new toys? You can do it if you learn everything you can.

STRAW BRIDGES TO THE FUTURE

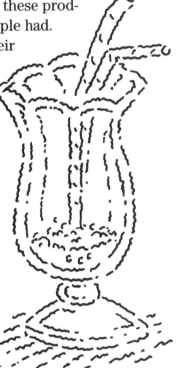

Every day we use the products of inventive minds. Some of these products came from trying to meet an important need that people had. Many, however, resulted from inventors trying to make their own lives a little more pleasant. One such product is the drinking straw.

If you wanted to make a drinking straw, how would you do it? There are no moving parts and no need for electricity, so it should be easy, right? How would you do it? . . . Well, maybe it's not so easy.

The drinking straw wasn't a product anyone needed. No one was asking for straws. Some people were using hollow reeds to suck up drinks, but the reeds added a distinctive taste to drinks, a taste that wasn't desired. Most people didn't bother using these reed straws.

This doesn't sound like a fertile field for an inventor to invest his or her time in. There was an existing product, but few people used it. Who would bother to invent something better?

Marvin Stone would. Not for the potential profit of making and selling straws, Stone wasn't interested in that. He just wanted his favorite drink to taste better when he drank it through a straw. So he rolled paper to make straws for himself.

Can you imagine what happened next? What would other people do when they saw Stone drinking through a paper straw?

Friends who saw Stone using his straws wanted some for themselves, so Stone started making them. He owned a factory that made paper products, so it was easy for him to have straws made. However, each straw had to be made by hand. For sixteen years workers wound paper around a form and glued the ends to make straws. Then, in 1906, another inventor made a machine to make straws, and the machine was able to make the straws at a lower cost. The straw industry grew rapidly after that.

Marvin Stone had not foreseen that he would start an entirely new industry. He had not set out to make money. He just wanted his favorite drink to taste better, so he tackled the problem and found a solution.

Since no one can predict the future, you can't tell if the things you invent will be great successes, like Marvin Stone's straws, or not. So a rule to follow is to make sure that you like your invention. If other people like it too, you might be able to sell it. If they don't like it, at least you can enjoy it.

TAKE-APART KING

One of the world's greatest inventors began his inventing career taking machines apart. Charles Kettering held 140 patents, had a town named after him (Kettering, Ohio) and started, with Alfred Sloan, a world-famous cancer research institute (the Sloan-Kettering Institute for Cancer Research). Not bad for a farm boy who liked to look inside machinery.

We remember Kettering for his contributions to the electrically operated cash register and accounting machines, and for his many inventions, including the self-starter for cars, four-wheel brakes for cars, freon for refrigerators, antiknock additives for gasoline, and safety glass.

Can you find Ohio on the map? Kettering did most of his work in Dayton, Ohio. Who can find that? How about finding Kettering, Ohio? It's near Dayton.

As a farm boy, Kettering was always tinkering and trying things. One day his family bought a new sewing machine for his mother. Sewing machines were very expensive then, and his family had saved money for a long time to be able to buy it. Sewing machines have many moving parts inside and aren't the sort of thing that someone should mess around with. Imagine his parents' horror when they walked into a room to find the sewing machine taken apart. Parts were everywhere.

Would you take apart something that was brand new? You shouldn't.

His parents asked him why he took it apart, and Charles told them that he wanted to learn how it worked.

Imagine the trouble he would have been in if he hadn't been able to get it back together. Would his parents have been angry with him? Charles must have learned how it worked because he was able to put it back together. He must have been the take-apart king.

Kettering had to drop out of school for a while because reading gave him headaches. But he learned at home and while working for a telephone company. He got back into college and became an electrical engineer.

He worked for the National Cash Register (NCR) company before starting his own business, the Dayton Engineering Laboratories Company or DELCO. After several years of operating the business, he sold it to General Motors. Today we call Kettering's business DELCO, and the people at DELCO still make parts for General Motors cars.

Kettering's biggest invention was the self-starter. What is a self-starter?

Before Kettering invented the self-starter, people had to start an engine with a hand crank. It required a strong person to do that, so unless someone was strong they didn't drive cars. And even strong people got hurt—in a few cases even killed—by trying to hand-start a car.

Kettering never believed anything until he tried it or tested it. If it didn't sound right to him, he would challenge a fact with experiments. Many times he found he was right and the experts were wrong.

Kettering went on to become one of the most successful inventors of all time. He liked to tell people that to be a successful inventor, the first thing to do is to stop worrying about making a mistake.

Why is it important in science and inventing not to worry about mistakes? (If you worry about mistakes, you won't try new things, and only by trying new things do you learn and make progress.) When shouldn't you make mistakes? (When someone's health or life could be endangered or when a mistake will hurt someone or something.)

When he died in 1958, he left his fortune to charity to help other people.

THE BATTLE OF THE CURRENTS

When you plug in an electric light or the toaster or television at home, you are using alternating current. When you turn on a flashlight or a portable radio, however, you are using direct current. At the start of the age of electricity, a battle waged between proponents of each current system, and the biggest name in technology, Thomas Edison, lost.

Do you know what alternative current and direct current are? What is the difference between them? (In direct current, the voltage put out by a battery remains constant. With alternating current, the voltage changes from positive to negative and back again sixty times a second. Wave your hand in an undulating fashion to show AC and hold it level to show DC.)

Edison's invention of the improved light bulb in 1879 led him to envision and then create an entire electrical system, starting with the generation of electricity, getting it to homes and businesses and making the electrical appliances used in homes and businesses. He wanted his company to sell you electricity, the lightbulbs and electric motors that used it, and the wires used to get it to you. Edison was trying to build an electrical empire.

Edison built his system around direct current or DC Motors that ran on DC already had been invented and Edison held patents on DC generators to make electricity. So Edison wanted to limit electrical usage to DC. However, there were problems with DC—copper wires needed to carry DC currents were costly, and the DC current couldn't travel very far. To supply people with electricity, Edison's company was going to have to build a power plant every two miles or so.

Imagine having a power plant every two miles. That would mean there would be one near you wherever you went. Since electricity was generated by burning coal, coal trucks would be rumbling by your house all the time.

People didn't like having power plants next to their houses. The plants were dirty since they burned coal—coal ash was always around and the air was dirty from smoke.

While Edison was building his electrical system, George Westinghouse was creating a different system, one based on alternating current or AC. When someone invented a way to get AC current to travel many miles through wires, Westinghouse bought the patent and started building his system.

Where is the electricity generated that we are using here? If we had Edison's DC system, the electrical generators would be within a few miles of us. With AC, there is no problem in getting the electricity to move long distances.

Even though many engineers agreed that Westinghouse's system was more practical, Edison fought against it. He said it was unsafe, that AC power was too dangerous to have in a home. Edison tried to scare people away from using AC power; he almost succeeded.

Another great inventor, Nikola Tesla, came to the rescue. Tesla invented an electric motor that ran on AC, and he sold it to Westinghouse. Now Westinghouse had a better system that could operate less expensively than Edison's.

Westinghouse won the war of currents when his company won the contract to build the world's first hydroelectric generating plant at Niagara Falls, New York. From that time on, we have used alternating current throughout America. Edison retreated from the war of currents and returned to his laboratory to continue his career as the world's most prolific and successful inventor.

THE MOST POPULAR FOUR-WHEEL VEHICLE

This is a story about a machine you have used many times. It has four wheels and can carry hundreds of pounds, but it doesn't have an engine. If you go to a supermarket you can find many of them. What is the machine? (A shopping cart.)

Today it seems obvious that people would use shopping carts when buying groceries, but before 1936 there were no shopping carts. People carried their purchases in hand baskets, and when the baskets were full or too heavy to carry any more, they would go to the checkout counter. This wasn't a problem because most of the stores were small and people were used to carrying all the purchases they wanted in a basket.

Can you imagine how much harder that would be to have to carry all your groceries while you shop?

Many inventions start with a need or a desire, and shopping carts were started with a need. A man named Sylvan Goldman owned several grocery stores in Oklahoma. He got the idea of making a shopping cart.

Let's find Oklahoma on the map. Who knows where it is?

Why do you suppose Mr. Goldman wanted to invent a shopping cart? (He wanted to sell more groceries, so he wanted to make it easier for his customers to pick up more goods and get them to the checkout counter.)

Mr. Goldman had the store handyman attach wheels to the legs of a folding chair. Then the handyman attached two baskets to the chair, and the result was a mock-up of a shopping cart.

Here is a folding chair. Imagine what it would look like with wheels and baskets. Would it look like a shopping cart? Can you imagine all the changes that people have made to the shopping cart since then?

Mr. Goldman had several shopping carts made, and he put them in one of his stores.

What do you imagine happened? Do you think people used them? (No. People don't change their habits that quickly.)

To get people to use his carts, Mr. Goldman hired some actors to push full carts around his store. That way customers got the idea of how they could use the carts. Then he hired someone to offer carts to customers as they entered his store. Once he showed customers how to use them, they did.

The shopping cart became so popular that two things happened. First, Mr. Goldman started a new company to build and sell shopping carts. Second, with big shopping carts, storeowners could make their stores bigger and carry more goods. Stores got larger, eventually becoming "supermarkets." Oh, one more thing happened. Mr. Goldman became one of the richest people in the United States.

Mr. Goldman solved a problem he had: how to enable customers to purchase more goods. His solution changed the way people buy and sell groceries.

Do you have some ideas of problems you could solve? What are they?

THE QUEST FOR SYNTHETIC RUBBER

The quest for new discoveries can lead inventors to some very strange results. Like Silly Putty®.

During World War II, the United States faced a shortage of rubber. The government contracted with General Electric to come up with a way to make synthetic rubber using silicone. At the same time scientists at Dow Corning Corporation were working on similar projects. The teams at both General Electric and Dow Corning made the same discovery: by adding boric acid to silicone oil, they found a new material.

They tested the material and found that it oozed or flowed very slowly, but would bounce off the floor when dropped. It acted like solid rubber when bounced but changed its shape when squeezed. "What good was that?" they wondered.

If you made something new and didn't know what it was good for, what would you do?

The scientists at GE sent samples around the world to engineers and scientists asking if they could find a use for the stuff. It wasn't useful for making tires or as a substitute for other rubber products. No one could think of a use for it, but people liked to play with it.

If people like to play with it, what do you think a good use for it is?

In 1949 a toy store owner found out about the substance at a party. She included it in a toy catalog and called it Nutty Putty. Although it sold well, she decided not to keep selling it. Peter Hodgson, who worked with the storeowner, thought it could continue to sell so he bought the rights to it. He packaged it in plastic eggs and changed the name to Silly Putty.

Toy experts weren't impressed with Silly Putty. They thought there was no future for it. But the toy experts were wrong. Since 1950 well over 200 million eggs of Silly Putty have been sold. About 2 million more are sold every year. It's even been in outer space—astronauts used it on *Apollo 8* to stick things to the spacecraft to keep them from flying around. What started as research to find a replacement for rubber produced one of the most popular toys of the century.

Are the experts always right? (No, even experts can be wrong.) That doesn't mean you shouldn't listen to them, but inventors have to make up their own minds.

THE WRIGHT STUFF

Each day hundreds of airplanes carrying people pass overhead. So do airplanes carrying packages and mail. Other planes are used by the military for defense of the country. All of them owe their origin to two brothers.

Do you know who the two brothers were?

Wilbur and Orville Wright. We call them the Wright Brothers because they worked together. They made the first airplane to fly with its own engine.

But the Wright Brothers didn't start out making airplanes. As boys Orville and Wilbur made mechanical toys to sell to other children. Later they started a printing business by making their own press, and the boys worked together to make a newspaper. A few years later they started in the bicycle business.

They got interested in flight and read everything they could find. One thing they learned was that a good place to test gliders and planes was on the coast of North Carolina at Kill Devil Hill.

Who knows what the difference is between a glider and an airplane? Can you make a model glider?

In 1900 they tested their first glider that carried a person. The following year they returned to Kill Devil Hill with a larger glider and continued their tests. They found that it didn't fly as well as they thought it would. When they went home to Ohio that year they decided to build a wind tunnel to help them understand why it hadn't flown well.

What is a wind tunnel? Could you build one out of a cardboard box and a fan?

Using the wind tunnel they discovered that much of the information published in books about wings of gliders was wrong. They conducted hundreds of tests to get better information, and with this information they were able to build a much better glider.

They went back to Kill Devil Hill in 1902 and flew the improved glider more than 1,000 times. It flew better than any other glider, and they got a patent for their improvements to the wings.

What is a patent? (A patent is a grant from the government that lets you, and only you, profit from the invention.)

With their improved glider the Wright Brothers decided to try making an airplane. In 1903 they returned to North Carolina and, on December 17, made the first powered flight. The Wrights kept working on new designs for planes and started a company to make them.

Of all the great inventors in the world, Wilbur and Orville Wright are among the most famous.

Why do you think the Wright Brothers succeeded when many other people failed? (Intelligent and persistent, they helped each other. They were willing to question the facts everyone else assumed were true.)

Let's look at a map to see where they lived and worked. Who can find the state of Ohio? Where is Dayton in Ohio? Now, where is North Carolina? Let's find Kill Devil Hill.

WHERE DOES IT HURT?

Who has used Band-Aids® to protect a cut? Band-Aids, like everything else we use, were invented. Can you imagine what led an inventor to make Band-Aids?

Josephine led an inventor to make Band-Aids. She was the young bride of cotton buyer, Earle Dickson, and she was clumsy in the kitchen. While preparing meals she cut herself with knives and burned herself on hot pots and pans. Then she would call Earle to come put bandages on the cuts and burns. Not having Band-Aids, Earle would place a sterile piece of cotton on the wound and, while trying to hold it steady, secure it with a piece of adhesive tape.

Earle thought there had to be a better way to protect cuts and bruises. In 1920 he took a piece of surgical tape and attached some cotton to the middle. By leaving the ends of the tape exposed, it would stick to the skin while holding the cotton gauze in place. Now Josephine could apply the Band-Aids herself when Earle wasn't home.

Do you think that a company would be interested in making a product like Band-Aids that no one had ever heard of before? Would the company be concerned that people wouldn't know what to do with a new product and wouldn't buy it?

Earle, it turns out, worked for a company by the name of Johnson & Johnson. Three brothers, named Johnson, had started the company in the 1880s to make and sell cotton dressings in germ-resistant packages. Before they started making these, people were dressing wounds with sawdust from wood mills. So the company was in the business of making sterile dressings and selling them in packages.

A fellow worker persuaded Earle to show his invention to his bosses. They liked the idea and started making Band-Aids. Initially sales were slow, but the company promoted Band-Aids heavily. They gave away samples to Boy Scouts and to butchers. With a strong promotion, sales eventually took off and Band-Aids became an important product for the company. Since their introduction in 1921, more than 100 billion Band-Aids have been used around the world.

Johnson & Johnson has earned a lot of money by making and selling Band-Aids. Earle was successful with the company and became a vice president. We don't know what happened to Josephine, but we imagine she too remained a big fan of Band-Aids.

What would you do if you had an idea for a new product? Would you take it to a company that made similar products? Would you get a patent for it?